# LAST APACHE REUNION

FORTY-FOUR SYCAMORE

# BERNARD FARRELL

# FORTY-FOUR, SYCAMORE

&

# THE LAST APACHE REUNION

MERCIER PRESS

MERCIER PRESS
PO Box 5, 5 French Church Street, Cork
16 Hume Street, Dublin 2


© Bernard Farrell, 1995
ISBN 1 85635 124 6


10  9  8  7  6  5  4  3  2  1

*A CIP record for this book is available from the British Library.*

The Publishers gratefully acknowledge the financial assistance of
The Arts Council/An Chomhairle Ealaíon

*Printed in Ireland by Colour Books Ltd.*

# CONTENTS

PREFACE            7

FORTY-FOUR, SYCAMORE     9

THE LAST APACHE REUNION     95

APPENDIX     187

# PREFACE

The song-writer, Sammy Cahn, was once asked 'which comes first – the words or the music?' He replied: 'First comes the phone call.' I may be able to go one better with *Forty-Four Sycamore*. Before a word had been written, Jim Nolan not only made a phone call but also penned a letter!

Jim was Artistic Director of Red Kettle, a theatre company that I greatly admired. In 1991, I had travelled to Waterford to see one of their excellent productions and, next day, came the phone call. Then came the letter. Both said the same thing: if I would consider writing a play, they would consider commissioning it.

At the time, I was involved in a television series – but I said an immediate 'yes', provided they could wait. They, in turn, not only promised to wait, but committed themselves to an Opening in Waterford, a transfer to Dublin and a National Tour. And all before a word had been written.

With such (frightening) trust in me, I was rocketed into exploring what the play could be about – and I constantly returned to the trials and tribulations of a couple moving into a new up-market estate.

Then I remembered a friend telling me how he and his new wife had once invited all the 'important people' to dinner and, within fifteen minutes, a silence descended and they knew they were in for an excruciating four hours. At one point, he escaped out to his back garden where he stood alone in the dark, wishing everyone would just go home, but knowing that there was no way he could escape returning to the horrors of the night.

Somehow, the image that came to mind was The Garden of Gethsemane – and, in that moment, I knew that the play would be about an appalling dinner party, an uninvited guest and the sheer fun-and-terror of a young couple trying to survive.

The play was written and delivered, the director was the

best director in Ireland for this kind of comedy, Paul Brennan, and I was delighted when it achieved its success in Waterford, Dublin *and* on tour.

My plan then was to write another play for Red Kettle – but Garry Hynes, Artistic Director of the Abbey, had already (over an excellent dinner) asked me if I had a play for them and I (surprising myself) told her that I knew exactly what the play would be about and when I would have it written.

This reflects the frightening nature of play-writing: some plays have to be excavated while others just lie waiting for the Time and Place. Garry provided both – and *The Last Apache Reunion* began.

I now know that I desperately wanted to write a single stage play about schooldays, macho deceptions and guilty secrets. All seemed to come together once I realised that the Reunion would take place in the original classroom, on a stormy night, just before the school was demolished. Now, not only could the Reunion involve the men of today, but also the ghosts of the past.

Ben Barnes directed the play at the Abbey (and thereafter) with a genuine feel for both the comedy and the terror ... and then (as in the cycle of life) I began my second play for Red Kettle ... and so it continues.

If 'bargaining' is an aspect of this business (and it must be), then I thank Jim Nolan for luring me back to the theatre and Garry Hynes for inviting me back to the Abbey. And, for my part of the bargain, I'm delighted that these two plays worked so well and justified the faith that was placed in me. The hope now, with this publication, is that I may continue to keep my bargain to future theatre companies and to all new audiences.

BERNARD FARRELL

# FORTY-FOUR, SYCAMORE

*This play was first produced by Red Kettle Theatre Company at Garter Lane Theatre Waterford on 4 February 1992 with the following cast:*

| | |
|---|---|
| VINNY | Tom Murphy |
| JOAN | Rachel Dowling |
| DEREK | Malcolm Douglas |
| HILARY | Hilary Fannin |
| PRENTICE | Des Braiden |

| | |
|---|---|
| DIRECTOR | Paul Brennan |
| DESIGNER | Ben Hennessy |
| LIGHTING | Roger Frith |

## *FOR GLORIA*

*Vinny and Joan's lounge in their new detached house on Sycamore Estate. It is evening. Door from hall is S/L. Door to the kitchen is upstage right. A large window at the back with a venetian blind, slats open, showing a green glow outside. The furniture includes a console which houses an electronic unit with many lights and switches. Also a stereo unit and a drinks cabinet.*

*We notice the amount of electric gadgetry in the room: speakers, spots, security lights, telephones (olde-world, decorative models) and a security TV monitor in the back wall. (Ideally, this monitor should be concealed behind a wall-panel and only revealed as required.) All gadgetry neatly installed. Vinny is 23, dressed in a suit – the jacket now off. He seems assured. He is busily (and proudly) blending his elaborate lighting system, using a remote control that he points at the console. Lights change tastefully across the room. Then all the phones tinkle – indicating that someone is dialling-out somewhere in the house. Vinny notices this with irritation.*

*Pause. Then Joan comes from the kitchen with bowls of crisps. She is 21, glamorous, in a rather short, attractive party-dress. She will nervously nibble at the crisps as she adjusts the furniture for the umpteenth time.*

| | |
|---|---|
| **Vinny:** | *(Easily)* Were you phoning your mother again? |
| **Joan:** | When now? |
| **Vinny:** | Thought I heard the phones tinkling. |
| **Joan:** | Oh yes. She was engaged. Just wanted to tell her how all the preparations is going. |
| **Vinny:** | *(Corrects) Are* going. *(Of the lights)* So what do you think? |
| **Joan:** | Don't make it too comfortable – they're only coming for 'drinks'. |
| | *(Vinny presses buttons on his remote control)* |
| **Vinny:** | I'll make the garden blue. |
| | *(The garden light changes to blue)* |
| **Joan:** | *(Anxiously)* You did say drinks, didn't you? |
| **Vinny:** | Did indeed. |
| **Joan:** | They better not think they're coming for a sit-down meal ... |

**Vinny:**   No – 'drinks' was the word. 'Come over for drinks – bring the wife and meet the wife.'

**Joan:**    Well I only hope they don't come in carrying a bottle of Blue Nun and thinking I've prepared ...

**Vinny:**   (*Laughs*) Blue Nun? Derek and Hilary would be more likely to come in carrying a bottle of Dom Perignon or ...

**Joan:**    (*Angrily*) They shouldn't come in carrying a bottle of anything if they're only coming for drinks!

**Vinny:**   (*Reacts*) I know that, Joan! I'm only saying that if they weren't coming for drinks, that's what they would be carrying but, as they are, they won't. (*More calm*) You'll like Derek – a great guy, life and soul of the squash club. *And* a doctor. *And* big in the Residents' Association. Very influential is our Derek.

**Joan:**    Well I don't know him.

**Vinny:**   Joan, you have to show interest, get out of the house, contribute. Otherwise we'll be another six months in the estate before we know anyone.

**Joan:**    I know Mr Prentice.

**Vinny:**   He's not in the estate.

**Joan:**    He is.

**Vinny:**   He's up in that big house, on his own and he's not liked! And you should have told me before you invited him. Supposing he doesn't get on with Derek and Hilary?

**Joan:**    He gets on with me.

**Vinny:**   But why?

**Joan:**    My ma says it's because he's lonely ...

**Vinny:**   Which is a great reason for *not* inviting him. We're trying to make important contacts here, Joan, not set up a branch of the Samaritans. (*Looks*) And I'd go easy on the crisps.
             (*Joan angrily pushes the crisps away*)

**Joan:**    What did you tell this Derek you were when he said he was a doctor?

**Vinny:**   He didn't actually say he was a doctor. In the

club, the word just gets around.

**Joan:** Well you should make sure that the word gets around that you're a security engineer. It sounds better. And my ma thinks so too.

**Vinny:** (*Ignores this. Hopefully*) Yes, tonight should be very impressive indeed.

**Joan:** As long as we don't have any of them big long silences.

**Vinny:** (*Annoyed*) Joan!

**Joan:** Well we could have!

**Vinny:** (*Corrects*) *Those* big long silences.

**Joan:** What?

**Vinny:** It's 'pardon' not 'what' – and you said 'any of *them* big long silences'.

**Joan:** Them or those, I won't be able to stick it if there is one.

**Vinny:** There won't be one if everyone contributes. Contributing is the art of conversation. And now you've eaten a whole bowl of crisps!

**Joan:** (*Picks it up*) All right!

**Vinny:** No sense in serving crisps and then having none for our guests.

**Joan:** I said 'all right'!

(*Joan takes the empty bowl into the kitchen. Vinny adjusts his lights. Then the phones tinkle again. Vinny notices this with annoyance – but then, a sudden 'bleep' is heard and a red light flashes on the wall. He quickly pulls on his jacket as he goes to the intercom on the wall and presses the 'kitchen' button. A buzzer is heard, off*)

**Vinny:** Joan, are you receiving me?

**Joan:** (*v/o*) What.

**Vinny:** (*Corrects*) Pardon! I'm getting a red flash here.

**Joan:** (*v/o*) It's not them already, is it?

**Vinny:** I'll check the monitor ...

**Joan:** (*v/o*) Okay – and Vinny ...?

**Vinny:** And I'll activate the outside security lights ...

**Joan:** (*v/o*) Okay – and Vinny ...?

**Vinny:**   ... and Joan, there's no time now for ringing your mother. Over and out.
*(Vinny rushes to the red light/bleep and turns it off. Takes the remote control and presses a series of buttons. The blue light outside changes to a dazzling white. Presses another button – and the TV monitor is automatically revealed from behind the wall panel. In black-and-white, we see a car come up to the house. This as Joan comes anxiously in, carrying a bowl of crisps)*

**Joan:**   Vinny? Listen Vinny ...

**Vinny:**   Hold on!

**Joan:**   Vinny, I meant to tell you ...

**Vinny:**   That's them – that's Derek's Volvo ...
*(He presses a button. A wall-panel automatically conceals the monitor again)*

**Joan:**   Vinny, listen ...

**Vinny:**   *(Checking)* Drinks over there ... glasses in place ...

**Joan:**   I meant to tell you before – but one of them ornamental elephants in the hall is broke and ...

**Vinny:**   *(Sudden anger)* Joan, for Christ's sake, one of *those* elephants is broken!

**Joan:**   *(Sudden anger)* There's no need to correct me if you know what I mean!
*(The door-bell chimes melodiously)*

**Vinny:**   There they are – are you all set?

**Joan:**   Did you hear what I said about ...?

**Vinny:**   Yes, I'll move the bloody thing – are you all set?

**Joan:**   Why are you snapping at me?

**Vinny:**   Right, if you're ready, I'll let them in. Soon as you hear the door close, turn the light back to blue and put the stereo on with ...

**Joan:**   You know I'm no good at them things ...
*(Vinny furiously presses the remote control)*

**Vinny:**   For God's sake: this switch is 'Off' – the light colours are numbered – could anything be easier ...?
*(The outside light goes from white to blue)*

|         | Now all you have to do is press these two together and the music comes on – and don't tell me you can't do that! |
|---------|---|

**Joan:** *(Suddenly in tears)* It's not my fault if I'm no good at this ...

**Vinny:** *(Stops. Suddenly calm, patient. Holds Joan)* It's all right, love – I know, I know – I'm sorry I snapped at you. Please don't get upset ...

**Joan:** *(Sobbing)* This is going to be awful ...

**Vinny:** No, it's not ...
*(The door-bell rings again)*

**Joan:** *(Crying)* I hate living here and I'm going to let you down and ruin your business chances ...

**Vinny:** No, you're not ...

**Joan:** I can't do anything ... I can't contribute ...

**Vinny:** You can – you can contribute with Mr Prentice ...

**Joan:** *(Indicates)* But *them!*

**Vinny:** If you can't contribute with them, just be agreeable – until someone else contributes – being agreeable is the secret of conversation.
*(The door-bell rings again)*

**Joan:** *(Calmer)* All right – I'll do my best.

**Vinny:** That's it. And anyway, I know how to handle these people – leave it all to me. They don't call me Mr Fix-It for nothing.
*(Anxious to go)*

**Joan:** *(Gently)* We were right to move here, Vinny, weren't we?

**Vinny:** *(Patiently)* Course we were.

**Joan:** Like they were friendlier where we were – near my ma and all.

**Vinny:** But we've moved up in the world, Joan – and aren't we the envy of them all – living here in Sycamore Estate?

**Joan:** I suppose so.

**Vinny:** Course we are. Now, those two buttons when you hear the door closing ...
*(The door-bell rings vigorously. Vinny going)*

| | |
|---|---|
| **Joan:** | All right – and you won't forget the elephant that's broke. *(Vinny stops – but decides not to correct her)* |
| **Vinny:** | I won't. |

*(Vinny goes. Joan presses the two buttons on the remote control. Wrong combination. The outside-window light goes rapidly from blue to red to white to blue. She panics. Voices are heard outside as she presses more buttons. The lights in the room dance. Panic as she presses more buttons. The lights dim low, the music comes on at high speed, an alarm bell begins to ring and a dazzling white light hits the door ... as Derek and Hilary enter, ahead of Vinny.*

*Both are 27, both very assured. Hilary in tasteful casuals. Derek looks very professional in a suit. Both now blinded by the spot-light)*

| | |
|---|---|
| **Hilary:** | *(Blinded)* Oh my God ... |

*(Vinny hurries in. Snaps the remote control from Joan)*

| | |
|---|---|
| **Vinny:** | Sorry – just a slight adjustment ... |
| **Joan:** | I couldn't manage ... |
| **Vinny:** | *(Angrily)* It's all right ... |
| **Derek:** | *(Still blinded. Merrily)* Anyone out there? |

*(Vinny presses the buttons. The room-lights become normal, the alarm stops, the music is soft and gentle.*

| | |
|---|---|
| **Hilary:** | Oh that's better ... |
| **Vinny:** | It's a burglar device actually ... |
| **Derek:** | *(Getting his vision back)* And a good one – a blind burglar can't do much harm. |
| **Vinny:** | Exactly – and we have the dogs as well. |
| **Hilary:** | We didn't see any dogs. |
| **Vinny:** | You'll meet them later. But now, I'd like you to meet my wife, Joan. Joan, Derek and Hilary from Sycamore Grove – the big houses at the top with the double garages. |
| **Joan:** | Oh yes. *(Hand out)* Hello Hilary. |
| **Hilary:** | Lovely to meet you, Joan. *(Kisses her)* |
| **Derek:** | *(Kisses Joan)* Great to meet you, Joan. |

**Joan:** Hello Derek. Hope you had no trouble finding us?

**Derek:** Not with your address.

**Hilary:** We think forty-four Sycamore sounds so wonderful.

**Joan:** Oh thank you.

**Hilary:** And your house is really lovely ... *(Looks)* with your lovely olde-world telephones ...

**Joan:** We got them specially ...

**Vinny:** Our policy is to mix the old style with the new ...

**Derek:** Absolutely – and that picture out in your hall is very stylish indeed.

**Hilary:** Of the horses – it's really fabulous.

**Joan:** *(Trying)* The one of them all galloping?

**Derek:** Yes – a very stylish painting.

**Joan:** We have another, nearly the same, in our master bedroom.

**Derek:** Have you really?

**Vinny:** *(Trying)* Except, in that one, the horses are all galloping in the other direction ...

**Joan:** And there's more of them ...

**Vinny:** That's right – and some of them are jumping. *(To Derek)* You see, both of us just love collecting pictures of horses.

**Joan:** I think they look so wild and, at the same time, they have such lovely faces and real sad eyes.

**Hilary:** You don't actually own any, do you?

**Joan:** Oh yes, we have three.

**Hilary:** Do you really?

**Joan:** Yes.

**Hilary:** And where do you keep them?

**Joan:** Well, there's the one hanging in the hall and there's another in the master bedroom and we have a little one out in the kitchen.

**Hilary:** No, no, real horses.

**Joan:** Real horses? Oh no, we've no real horses.

**Vinny:** *(Laughing it off)* And certainly not in our master bedroom.

**Derek:**   *(Laughing it off)* Nor hanging in the hall.

**Hilary:**   *(Laughing it off)* Or in the kitchen.

**Vinny:**   No. Very good. Yes. *(An awkward moment)*

**Hilary:**   *(Prompting)* Derek ...?

**Derek:**   *(Aroused)* Oh yes, of course. *(Goes towards the door)* Left it outside – the shock of seeing Vinny holding two elephants. *(Derek goes outside)*

**Hilary:**   *(To Joan)* Vinny had a handful of elephants when he opened the door.

**Joan:**   *(Merrily)* Had he really?

**Derek:**   *(Coming in)* Now Joan. Hope I got it right. It's red. *(He gives Joan a bottle of wine)*

**Hilary:**   Don't worry, Joan – if it should be white, if you're serving fish tonight, just keep it for another time.

**Derek:**   *(Laughs)* It's only vinegar anyway.

**Vinny:**   *(Bravely)* Not if I know you, Derek, not if I know you. Many thanks indeed. Now, what are we all drinking?
*(Joan holds the wine aghast)*

**Derek:**   *(Laughs)* I can see I got it wrong, Joan.

**Vinny:**   No no ...

**Derek:**   But you can blame me – Hilary said bring white because it's Friday and it could be fish but I must confess I'm a meat man myself.

**Hilary:**   Derek, you like fish.

**Derek:**   Oh anything on a plate for Derek.

**Vinny:**   Talking of which, Derek – well of glasses not plates – I think I saw you drinking Bushmills at the club?

**Derek:**   *(Sitting)* Well observed, Vinny.

**Vinny:**   Thank you, Derek – and coming up. *(Goes to the drinks)*
*(Joan would follow Vinny for protection)*

**Hilary:**   *(Sits)* Your kitchen is out there, is it, Joan?

**Joan:**   What? *(Corrects)* Pardon?

**Hilary:**   In our houses – and in Sycamore Downs and Sycamore Lawns – the kitchen is over there. *(Opposite)*

**Joan:** (*Stunned*) Is it?

**Vinny:** (*Covering up*) Oh yes, remember we looked at that showhouse – beautiful houses, magnificent lay-out.

**Hilary:** We like them. But Amanda and Tony have one of these, haven't they, Derek?

**Derek:** Amanda and Tony, yes – in forty-eight Sycamore.

**Vinny:** (*Trying hard*) Oh yes, a lovely couple.

**Hilary:** And you have the walk-in cloakroom, have you?

**Vinny:** No, we have the king-size sunken bath en suite in the master bedroom with the mahogany sur-round and the porcelain taps.

**Hilary:** That's funny – Amanda and Tony have the walk-in cloakroom.

**Derek:** I'd say they put that in, darling.

**Hilary:** Very likely. Not coming tonight, are they?

**Vinny:** Amanda and Tommy? No, they said they couldn't make it.

**Derek:** No, Amanda and Tony, in forty-eight.

**Vinny:** Oh, Amanda and Tony! No, they couldn't make it either. Now a Bushmills – and Hilary, I haven't forgotten you.

**Hilary:** Oh, nothing for me, Vinny – thanks.

**Vinny:** Nothing at all?

**Hilary:** No, honestly – I seldom drink before I eat.

**Vinny:** (*Bravely*) Right. Joan?

**Joan:** (*Stunned*) What?

**Vinny:** Pardon. What do you want to drink?

**Joan:** Vinny ... (*Looks like she might escape to the kitchen*)

**Vinny:** I know – you'll have a sherry. It's always a sherry for Joan. Hilary, are you sure?

**Hilary:** Well, if everyone is drinking, a glass of water then – from the tap – nothing fancy.

**Vinny:** No problem. I'll nip out and get that for you ...

**Joan:** (*Anxious to escape*) No, I'll get it ...

**Vinny:** Joan, I'll get it – I know exactly what to do ...

**Derek:** (*Merrily*) Turn on the tap, I presume!

**Vinny:** Exactly, Derek. (*To Joan*) And I'll check how

|        | dinner is coming along – just relax here ... |
|--------|--------|
| **Joan:** | But we've no ... |
| **Vinny:** | Just relax ... *(Going)* |
| **Derek:** | And maybe over dinner, Vinny, we could chat about your security system here. |
| **Vinny:** | *(Stops)* Oh certainly, Derek. |
| **Derek:** | It's very impressive – and could be what we need at the club. |
| **Vinny:** | A good system is always a sound investment, Derek. |
| **Hilary:** | Now Derek, don't turn this into another business dinner. |
| **Derek:** | *(Merrily)* Don't worry, love – we'll only mention it over the soup. |
| **Joan:** | *(Quiet panic)* Soup! |
| **Vinny:** | *(To Hilary)* Exactly. You're here to enjoy yourselves and we're here to see that you do. So, minimum business, maximum relaxation. |
| **Hilary:** | Thank you, Vinny. How many have you coming? |
| **Vinny:** | *(Awkwardly)* Apart from yourselves, do you mean? |
| **Hilary:** | Well yes – is it a big crowd? |
| **Vinny:** | No – in fact, we invited just one other person – didn't we, Joan? |
| **Joan:** | What? Pardon! Yes. |
| **Derek:** | Just one other apart from us? |
| **Vinny:** | We thought tonight we'd keep it nice and intimate, for a change. |
| **Derek:** | Well, I can tell you, that's all right with me. |
| **Vinny:** | Oh great. You probably know the other person who's coming – Mr Prentice: the old chap who lives up in Sycamore House ... |
| **Joan:** | The house with the big Sycamore tree outside it. |
| **Vinny:** | You might often see him walking around the estate, talking to everyone ... *(Both Derek and Hilary begin to laugh)* Do you know him – very thick glasses ...? |
| **Hilary:** | And that long coat in the winter? |

| | |
|---|---|
| **Vinny:** | That's right – that's him. |
| **Derek:** | *(Laughing)* And you've invited him here for dinner? |
| **Joan:** | For drinks. |
| **Vinny:** | No, dinner! |
| **Hilary:** | *(Laughing)* I think drinks would be wiser. |
| **Joan:** | Anyway, he said he'd be here after nine – he said he had something to do. *(Another burst of laughter from Derek and Hilary)* |
| **Derek:** | I wonder what that could be! |
| **Vinny:** | *(Lost)* We just thought we'd ask him because he's one of the older inhabitants here, probably knows the whole history of the place. |
| **Derek:** | *(Stops)* You're not serious, are you? |
| **Vinny:** | About what, Derek? |
| **Hilary:** | You haven't really invited him, have you? |
| **Derek:** | That was a joke, wasn't it? |
| **Vinny:** | A joke? No, we just asked him if he was doing nothing ... |
| **Derek:** | Good God, you *are* serious. |
| **Vinny:** | Well, it was really Joan ... |
| **Derek:** | Do you not know about him? |
| **Hilary:** | Now, Derek! |
| **Vinny:** | *(Catching on)* Well I heard rumours ... |
| **Derek:** | Rumours? It's more than rumours. Colm O'Reilly has enough on him to send him to jail! |
| **Hilary:** | Colm is very hot-headed. |
| **Derek:** | Colm's a county councillor, captain of the senior squash team – and since when is it hot-headed to confront someone who sends you anonymous letters and smears your car with cow-manure? |
| **Hilary:** | Nobody knows it was ... |
| **Derek:** | And what about him peeping in through bed-room windows at night? |
| **Hilary:** | Oh Derek! |
| **Derek:** | Colm says he has complaints from housewives all across the estate ... his wife calls him Prentice-the-Pervert. |

**Hilary:**  Now Colm's wife is ...

**Derek:**  And I don't see why you're suddenly defending him ...

**Hilary:**  I'm not – I just think he's more to be pitied ...

**Joan:**  That's what I think ...

**Derek:**  Pitied my arse! *(To Vinny)* Sorry Vinny, but I must be honest about your friend Prentice ...

**Vinny:**  He's not my friend, Derek ...

**Derek:**  I mean, you ask anyone in the whole estate ...

**Hilary:**  And they'll say he's peculiar ...

**Derek:**  They'll say he's most peculiar, a nuisance and, into the bargain, probably bent. How well do you actually know him, Vinny?

**Vinny:**  Me? I don't know him at all. It was Joan ...

**Joan:**  I usually see him whenever I ...

**Vinny:**  I even said to Joan that I never liked the look of him – didn't I say that, Joan?

**Joan:**  Yes, but ...

**Derek:**  Well fine, okay, I'll just say this and leave it at that: I'd think twice before I'd invite him to my house.

**Hilary:**  Derek, you can't tell people ...

**Vinny:**  No, Hilary, I take Derek's point – we both do – and we'll be only too delighted to put him off.

**Hilary:**  Oh there's no need ...

**Derek:**  Of course, if he's invited ...

**Vinny:**  But that's the point – he's not, not really – like it wasn't final. Is he on the phone, Joan?

**Joan:**  Mr Prentice?

**Vinny:**  *(Angrily)* Yes, Mr Prentice! – let me check that. *(Hurriedly gets a telephone directory)*

**Joan:**  Vinny, we can't ...

**Vinny:**  *(To Derek)* I suppose the point is you're longer in Sycamore Estate – like if the situation was reversed, we might know someone who you think might be grand when he might really be God-knows-what.

**Derek:**  Well, this is it, Vinny.

| | |
|---|---|
| **Hilary:** | *(To Joan)* Are you sure ...? |
| **Joan:** | Oh yes. |
| **Vinny:** | *(With the directory)* P... P... Prentice, Sycamore House – here he is. And thank you for tipping us off ... |
| **Derek:** | Colm O'Reilly has stories, going back years, about the goings-on of friend Prentice. |
| **Vinny:** | *(Writes down the number)* Tell you what – I'll phone him from the kitchen while I'm getting your water, Hilary. |
| **Joan:** | *(Moves)* I'll do it. |
| **Vinny:** | *(Firmly)* You chat to Derek and Hilary for a minute – I'll check-out all of this. Maybe pour me a Bushmills, like Derek's. *(Quietly angry to Joan, as he goes)* Contribute! |
| | *(Vinny hurries into the kitchen. Joan, abandoned and lost, sits)* |
| **Hilary:** | So now it'll be dinner for four. |
| **Joan:** | *(Decides)* Yes, four. |
| **Hilary:** | Nice even number. |
| **Joan:** | Yes. |
| | *(The phones tinkles – Vinny phoning out)* |
| **Derek:** | Fish? |
| **Joan:** | Pardon me? |
| **Derek:** | The red wine – sorry I didn't think of fish. |
| **Joan:** | Oh that's all right. |
| **Hilary:** | Joan, allow me to put your mind at ease – he absolutely loves fish ... |
| **Derek:** | Anything on a plate for Derek. |
| **Hilary:** | In fact, we both do ... so fish would be perfect. |
| **Joan:** | Oh, grand. |
| | *(Another silence. Then Derek is suddenly on his feet)* |
| **Derek:** | Now, I think I know Vinny's measure. |
| **Joan:** | *(Jumps up)* His what? |
| **Derek:** | *(Goes to the drinks)* Don't mind, do you? |
| **Joan:** | No – but I should be doing that. |
| **Hilary:** | You'll have enough to do later. |
| **Derek:** | Absolutely. Harvey's for you, Joan? |

**Joan:**      Yes, but really I should ...

**Hilary:**    We both love to pitch in when we're out visiting.
               *(Then)* And Vinny is in the security business?

**Joan:**      Oh yes – he's a security engineer, in fact.

**Derek:**     And wouldn't you know.

**Joan:**      He has his own business and all now and three
               branches – well only two now since ... well since
               Christmas, but it's going great.
               *(The phones tinkles – Vinny making another call)*

**Derek:**     Excellent. Now a Bushmills for Vinny, a sherry
               for you and a refill for moi.

**Joan:**      Oh thanks.

**Hilary:**    So now that we know that Vinny is a ...

**Joan:**      Security engineer.

**Hilary:**    Yes, would you like to guess what Derek is?

**Joan:**      Derek?

**Hilary:**    Yes, just looking at him now.

**Joan:**      He's a doctor, isn't he?
               *(Both Derek and Hilary laugh at this private joke. Joan
               is lost)*

**Hilary:**    *(To Derek, merrily)* I told you!

**Derek:**     *(To Hilary, merrily)* No – I know why she said that.

**Hilary:**    *(To Joan)* Do you think he looks like one?

**Derek:**     She saw it sticking out of my pocket.

**Hilary:**    No, let her say. *(To Joan)* Why did you think he
               was a doctor?

**Joan:**      Vinny told me he was.

**Derek:**     Did he really?

**Hilary:**    *(To Derek)* You see, he thought so too.

**Derek:**     No no, that was because I bandaged Geoffrey's
               ankle at the club.

**Hilary:**    *(To Joan)* Is that why Vinny said he was a doctor?

**Joan:**      No, I think the word just gets around.

**Derek:**     You didn't see it sticking out of my pocket?

**Joan:**      Pardon me?
               *(Derek takes a small stethoscope from his inside jacket
               pocket)*

**Derek:**     My stethoscope.

| | |
|---|---|
| **Hilary:** | Derek carries it everywhere. |
| **Derek:** | And a complete First Aid kit in the car: bandages, splints, surgical spirit, the lot. |
| **Hilary:** | Which is more than most doctors have ... |
| **Derek:** | Came in very handy when that boy fell off his bike ... |
| **Hilary:** | *(To Joan)* Derek had all his bandages out and a splint on while everyone else just stood around looking ... |
| **Derek:** | You have to think fast ... |
| **Hilary:** | ... and at the hospital, you should have heard him discussing the case with the doctor – I just stood back. *(To Derek)* He was certain you were another doctor. |
| **Derek:** | Think he realised I knew my stuff. |
| **Hilary:** | *(To Joan)* Every Thursday without fail, hail rain or shine, Derek is off to his First Aid class. |
| **Derek:** | Practice makes perfect. |
| **Joan:** | And he isn't really a doctor at all? |
| **Hilary:** | *(Confidentially)* When I was having Simon ... |
| **Derek:** | What an experience! |
| **Hilary:** | Simon was our first and Derek *insisted* on being with me in the delivery room, even though it was a Thursday. |
| **Derek:** | *(To Joan)* Was Vinny at any of yours? |
| **Joan:** | My what? |
| **Derek:** | Any of your deliveries. |
| **Joan:** | Oh no, no he wasn't actually because we don't have any children ... well not yet anyway ... |
| **Hilary:** | Oh shame, Joan. |
| **Joan:** | Though I did have two phantom pregnancies, both in the first year ... |
| **Hilary:** | Oh well, third time lucky, I'm sure. |
| **Joan:** | Well actually, we're not too bothered now, one way or the other. |
| **Derek:** | Well if you do – and I'm sure you will – you tell Vinny to be there. You insist he be there. |
| **Hilary:** | Does he do First Aid – Vinny? |

**Joan:**      No, he's a security engineer.

**Hilary:**      Well, if Vinny can't be there, Derek could be there – you could be there, Derek.

**Derek:**      Only if Joan and Vinny were agreeable ...

**Hilary:**      Of course they'd be agreeable. You'd be agreeable, Joan, wouldn't you?

**Joan:**      *(Agreeably)* Oh yes, of course ...

**Hilary:**      Very wise and I'll tell you why: if Derek wasn't at Simon's, he'd be a vegetable today.

**Joan:**      Derek would?

**Hilary:**      No, Simon – Simon would be a vegetable today if Derek hadn't been there at the delivery.

**Derek:**      What an experience!

**Hilary:**      I was half-unconscious, pushing hard and all that – but all I could hear was this voice positively screaming instructions and only after did I realise it was Derek screaming at the gynaecologist.

**Derek:**      They'd virtually cut off the child's air supply.

**Hilary:**      He'd be a vegetable today – and God only knows how many more have been delivered like that because no one pays attention.

**Joan:**      God. And you're not really a doctor at all?

**Derek:**      No – actually I'm in advertising. A lot of television contract work ...

**Hilary:**      But to everyone ...

**Derek:**      And I could be doing the advertising campaign for the next phase of Sycamore Estate ...

**Hilary:**      Yes – but to everyone, he's the doctor because he does look like one, don't you think?

**Joan:**      Oh definitely ...

**Hilary:**      And he'll look after you when your time comes – and it will, you'll see.

**Joan:**      Well, we're not really bothered, one way or the other.

     *(Vinny comes from the kitchen, very assured. He carries a glass of water)*

**Vinny:**      Here we are, Hilary.

**Derek:**      *(Merrily)* Vinny! Where did you go – the Syca-

| | more Oasis? |
|---|---|
| **Vinny:** | *(Joining in)* Very good. But always best to let the tap run, get it nice and cold. Sip that now, Hilary and tell me. |
| **Hilary:** | *(Sips)* Yes. Lovely. |
| **Vinny:** | Cold enough? We have an ice-bucket. |
| **Hilary:** | No no, perfect. |
| **Vinny:** | Excellent. *(Towards Joan)* And everything else is under control – nothing to worry about at all. |
| **Derek:** | You got him, did you? |
| **Vinny:** | Got who, Derek? |
| **Derek:** | Prentice. |
| **Vinny:** | Oh Prentice – no, the line was engaged, so he's still at home, so I'll get him again ... did he say nine, Joan? |
| **Joan:** | After nine. |
| **Vinny:** | Then plenty of time to divert him. |
| **Derek:** | Excellent – poured you a Bushmills ... |
| **Vinny:** | Excellent – and you have your sherry, Joan? |
| **Joan:** | Yes ... |
| **Vinny:** | Excellent and dinner, I'd say, in about an hour if that suits everybody? |
| **Hilary:** | Lovely. *(Hungrily takes a handful of crisps)* |
| **Vinny:** | Excellent. *(To Joan)* So what did I miss – what was the conversation, darling? |
| **Joan:** | Me? Oh Derek and .... |
| **Vinny:** | Hilary, yes. |
| **Joan:** | Hilary were telling me all about Simon. |
| **Hilary:** | It could have been a horror story, Vinny, if Derek hadn't been overseeing the delivery. |
| **Vinny:** | *(Lost)* Really? |
| **Joan:** | *(Trying)* They were saying it's very important to be always there because no one knows how many vegetables are being delivered every day the way things are done so carelessly. |
| **Vinny:** | *(Lost)* Is that a fact? |
| **Hilary:** | We've no way of knowing, Vinny. |
| **Derek:** | My advice is always make sure you are at every |

delivery, whether you fancy the idea or not.

**Vinny:** Well thanks, Derek, but luckily we grow our own.

**Derek:** Pardon?

**Vinny:** We've just a small vegetable plot beyond the lawn and we have some carrots and lettuce ...

**Joan:** *(Desperate)* No Vinny, it's Simon they're talking about.

**Vinny:** Simon? Who's Simon?

**Hilary:** Simon is our eldest child ...

**Derek:** Two years older than Rebecca ...

**Joan:** They were telling me how he was born – that was the vegetable they were talking about.

**Vinny:** Oh good God, my apologies – I'd no idea he was ...

**Hilary:** No, he's grand, he's fine ...

**Vinny:** But you just said he's ...

**Hilary:** No – if Derek hadn't been there at the delivery ...

**Derek:** ... his air-supply would have been cut off ...

**Hilary:** ... then he would have been a vegetable ...

**Derek:** But now he's perfect – brightest child in his class and came second in the toddler's race last week.

**Vinny:** Oh I see.

**Joan:** *(Annoyed)* That's what I meant.

**Vinny:** *(Assured)* Well that all goes to prove just one thing, doesn't it? – isn't it great, Hilary, that you're married to a doctor.

*(Again, both Hilary and Derek laugh delightfully at this notion)*

**Joan:** *(Quietly, anxiously)* He's not a doctor!

**Hilary:** *(To Vinny)* You really thought he was, didn't you?

**Vinny:** *(Trying to join in)* Well he is, isn't he?

**Hilary:** *(Merrily to Derek)* See? I told you.

**Joan:** *(Anxiously to Vinny)* He has a periscope sticking out of his pocket.

**Vinny:** What?

**Derek:** *(Merrily)* I never said I was you know.

**Hilary:** You don't need to, darling.

**Vinny:** *(Laughing along)* And you're not, are you not?

**Derek:**   No, I'm in advertising.

**Vinny:**   Advertising? But down in the club ...

**Hilary:**   *(Proudly)* Oh we know, Vinny, we know.

**Derek:**   And you may have seen this. *(Produces the stethoscope)* Take this everywhere.

**Joan:**   *(To Vinny)* There!

**Vinny:**   *(Angrily to Joan)* That's not a periscope!

**Hilary:**   No, it's called a stethoscope.

**Vinny:**   I know that, Hilary.

**Derek:**   A periscope is a thing on a submarine.

**Vinny:**   *(Trying to get off this)* I know, but some people get them confused – but you're really in advertising?

**Hilary:**   Yes, but medicine would always be his first love.

**Derek:**   *(To Vinny)* Do you know 'The Commodore bed is the bed to rely on'?

**Vinny:**   *(Lost)* Is it really?

**Derek:**   No, that's the ad on the telly – *(sings)* 'the Commodore bed is the bed to rely on ...' with the Polar Bears hopping up and down.

**Vinny:**   Oh that one, yes.

**Derek:**   *(Proudly)* Well that's mine.

**Joan:**   I think I saw that on a bus.

**Derek:**   *(Delighted)* Yes, and we've placed it in selected railway stations.

**Vinny:**   And you wrote it?

**Hilary:**   Yes, but medicine would always be his ...

**Derek:**   *(To Vinny)* Yes, all of that's mine – I can still remember the day I thought-up that bit: 'Lie on it', 'rely on it'.

**Vinny:**   Ah that's very clever.

**Derek:**   And now I've been promised the contract to do all the advertising for the new estate – up beyond the New Road ...

**Vinny:**   God, that's great, Derek – congratulations.

**Hilary:**   *(A point)* But despite all that, medicine would always be Derek's first love.

**Derek:**   *(Suddenly annoyed)* I'm not saying it's not, Hilary.

**Hilary:**   I'm merely saying if you had a choice ...

**Derek:**    I know what you're saying – I'm not deaf – I know!

**Hilary:**    *(Ending this, sharply)* All right!

**Vinny:**    *(Then, awkwardly)* Excellent.
*(An awkward silence. Derek hungrily takes a handful of crisps. So does Hilary)*

**Hilary:**    *(Lightly)* We mustn't eat too many and insult Joan's cooking.

**Derek:**    Indeed.

**Hilary:**    We were just saying, Vinny, that we both love fish.

**Vinny:**    Really? Joan, make a note of that for next time.

**Derek:**    Why – isn't it fish tonight?

**Vinny:**    Tonight? Here, you mean?

**Joan:**    *(Quickly)* Derek and Hilary were just saying ...

**Derek:**    No, I was really apologising for the red wine and ...

**Vinny:**    Oh don't be worrying about that, Derek. No, what we're having tonight, what we planned for tonight – and we hope it is to your taste, hope you're not allergic to them or anything – is pizzas.

**Hilary:**    Pardon?

**Vinny:**    Oh, do you not like them, Hilary?

**Hilary:**    No, no ....

**Derek:**    But Joan said it was fish tonight.

**Joan:**    *(Anxiously)* They kept asking me and I ...

**Vinny:**    *(Quickly)* ... and you didn't want to spoil our little surprise. Okay, so now you may as well know it all. We were hoping that you both like fish – you do, don't you – like fish?

**Derek:**    Well yes, or whatever ...

**Hilary:**    Doesn't really matter ...

**Vinny:**    What kind? Tuna? Tuna fish or maybe anchovies?

**Derek:**    Honestly, we're happy to have whatever Joan has prepared ...

**Joan:**    *(Anxiously)* Vinny ...

**Vinny:**    No, you're the guests, you say – tuna fish all right?

**Hilary:** Tuna fish would be lovely if ...
**Derek:** Yes, tuna ...
**Vinny:** Delighted to hear that because tuna is exactly what it is. Tuna pizzas for you both, Pineapple-and-Ham for Joan and I, all 12 inch, specially prepared by Joan and complete with coleslaw, garlic bread and a salad from our own garden. How does that sound?
**Hilary:** *(To Joan)* It sounds like too much trouble – doing separate dishes ...
**Vinny:** No, no, worth doing at all is worth doing well.
**Derek:** But how did you know we'd like fish?
**Vinny:** How did I know you drank Bushmills – observation. Talking of which, you'll go again?
**Derek:** Won't say no. *(Gives Vinny his glass)*
**Vinny:** And Joan, maybe you'd give Hilary a refill of water there.
**Hilary:** No, no, I'm fine.
**Vinny:** No, no, that must be warm by now – use the cold tap, Joan, let it run ...
**Hilary:** No, honestly ... *(Tries to hold her glass)*
**Vinny:** *(Takes her three-quarter full glass)* No dinner guest of our's will be drinking hot water, Hilary. *(To Joan, off-hand)* And there's a note on the table.
**Joan:** What note?
**Vinny:** *(Loudly)* And try ringing Prentice again. *(Quietly)* On the kitchen table *(Loudly)* ... and the cold tap for Hilary ... and I'll pour you another sherry here, all right?
*(The phones ring)*
**Vinny:** And I'll get that. *(Quietly)* Change the order to two tuna delivered around the back ... now!
*(Joan goes annoyed to the kitchen as Vinny picks up a phone)*
**Derek:** Mind if I put on some music?
**Vinny:** Sure Derek – CD's in alphabetical order and just press 3 and 5 together on the Remote Control.
*(As Derek goes to the stereo to choose music)*

*(Into phone)* Vinny O'Sullivan speaking. *(Then)* Oh hello, Betty. *(Hand over phone. To Derek)* Joan's mother. *(Into phone)* Very well indeed. *(Pause)* Well she's in the kitchen looking in at her excellent cooking. *(Pause)* Well we decided to after – Betty can I get her to call you back? *(Pause)* No, I don't think he is now – Betty I'll ask her to get back to you pronto. *(Pause)* Right, great, ciao.

*(As Vinny puts the phone down, Derek presses the Remote Control buttons. The music plays)*

| | |
|---|---|
| **Vinny:** | Joan's mother – likes to keep in touch. |
| **Hilary:** | I think that's lovely. |
| **Vinny:** | Yes, I always encourage it. |
| **Derek:** | She isn't a model, is she? |
| **Vinny:** | Joan's mother? |
| **Derek:** | No, Joan – she looks like a model. |
| **Hilary:** | Yes, she has a lovely figure. |
| **Vinny:** | No no, she's not – though everyone says she ought to be. |
| **Derek:** | Well absolutely. |

*(The phones tinkle – Joan dialling out)*

| | |
|---|---|
| **Vinny:** | Now, two Bushmills. *(Goes to the drinks)* |
| **Derek:** | Great. |
| **Vinny:** | And that is some surprise you not being a doctor, Derek. |
| **Derek:** | Surprises everybody, that. |
| **Hilary:** | Every Thursday, hail rain or shine, he's off to practice. |
| **Derek:** | Practice makes perfect. And your Joan passed me a lovely compliment. |
| **Vinny:** | Oh yes? *(Gives Derek his drink)* |
| **Derek:** | She said I could be present at her first. |
| **Vinny:** | Her first what, Derek? |
| **Hilary:** | Her first baby. |
| **Vinny:** | Baby? But she's not ... you know ... is she? |
| **Derek:** | *(Merrily)* Well you tell us! |
| **Vinny:** | No, that's what I mean, as far as I know – but did she tell you she was ...? |

**Hilary:** No, the poor thing just said she had two phantom pregnancies ...

**Vinny:** *(Controlled)* Oh mentioned those, did she ...?

**Hilary:** Yes, but we said that can be very disappointing but to keep on trying ...

**Derek:** And when the news is good and she's having her first, she said I could be there.

**Vinny:** Where, Derek?

**Derek:** At the delivery.

**Hilary:** Of her first little baby.

**Derek:** Agreed that it would put her at her ease to have me there, just looking on, keeping an eye on things.

**Vinny:** Oh right. And when she said this – that you could be there, keeping an eye on things – was that when she thought you *were* a doctor?

**Derek:** No, that was the great compliment – she said it when I told her I wasn't, had no hesitation whatsoever.

**Hilary:** You wouldn't mind, would you, Vinny?

**Vinny:** *(Bravely)* Mind? Why would I mind – isn't he almost a doctor anyway – all the fellows in the club say that.

**Hilary:** Exactly.

**Vinny:** *(Quietly and angrily towards the kitchen)* Jesus!
*(The phones tinkle again – Joan making another call)*

**Hilary:** And Joan was telling us that you are actually a security engineer.

**Vinny:** Oh indeed, yes.

**Derek:** *(Looking around)* As I said – very very impressive.

**Vinny:** Oh thank you, Derek.

**Derek:** And very necessary on this estate – we're too close to those bloody council houses for safety.

**Vinny:** Couldn't agree more, Derek – *(In his element)* though my personal, professional advice would be that your average domestic dwelling in an up-market estate such as Sycamore would not require such advanced technology as you see here –

in fact, most surveys suggest that your greatest house security is either your all-purpose sensor alarm system with a frequency to your local police station or, very simply, your average guard dog.

**Derek:** And you have a dog as well, do you?

**Vinny:** We have three – an Alsatian, a Doberman and a Rottweiler.

**Derek:** Good God.

**Hilary:** *(Merrily)* I'm glad we didn't know that coming in.

**Vinny:** Nothing to fear, Hilary, once you have them under control.

**Derek:** A well-trained dog is the secret, eh?

**Vinny:** Absolutely. Just let me turn off the outside alarms so they won't set them off ... *(Throws a wall switch)* and the lights ... *(Presses his remote control: the lights dim outside)* I'll show you. Don't say a word now. Just listen.

*(Vinny gives a gentle whistle. Immediately, ferocious barking and growling is heard outside, coming towards the window. It arrives and stays outside, loud and frightening)*

**Derek:** Jesus Christ!

**Vinny:** Now that's what burglars fear – that is your complete deterrent.

**Derek:** I believe you!

**Hilary:** Can they get in?

**Vinny:** *(Merrily)* Open the window and find out.

**Derek:** Christ – don't!

**Vinny:** It's okay, we won't.

**Derek:** That's an Alsatian and what?

**Vinny:** Doberman and Rottweiler. But well under control.

**Derek:** *(Laughs)* Glad to hear it.

**Vinny:** Trained to do everything – even to circle the house in a pack. Watch.

*(Vinny gives another distinctive whistle. The sound of the dogs fade from the window and we hear them*

*outside the hall-door)*

**Derek:** Where are they now?

**Vinny:** That was the front-door whistle.

**Derek:** They're now around at the front-door?

**Vinny:** Waiting for an intruder ... or an extruder!

**Hilary:** Can we go see them?

**Vinny:** Sure – look through the glass panels.

**Hilary:** Fabulous.

**Derek:** *(Going. Excited)* But they can't get in, can they?

**Vinny:** Just don't open the door.

**Hilary:** *(Going)* Don't worry – we won't.

**Derek:** *(Going)* This is excellent.

**Vinny:** *(Calls)* Just keep watching – let your eyes get used to the dark.

*(With Derek and Hilary gone, Vinny goes anxiously towards the kitchen – as Joan comes anxiously out)*

**Joan:** Oh God, this is awful.

**Vinny:** *(Angrily)* What about the pizzas?

**Joan:** You said they were only coming for drinks ...

**Vinny:** Are they delivering the pizzas to the back door or not?

**Joan:** Yes!

**Vinny:** Two tunas, twelve inches with coleslaw ...?

**Joan:** Yes, in five minutes – but you said they were only coming for drinks.

**Vinny:** And Prentice – did you get on to Prentice?

**Joan:** No – because my ma said we should let him come.

**Vinny:** Your ma?! How does your ma come into this?

**Joan:** I rang her to ask her...

**Vinny:** For Christ's sake, between you and your ma you're going to shaggin' ruin me with these people ...

**Hilary:** *(Off)* Vinny? Vinny?

**Vinny:** *(Calls)* Yes, Hilary?

*(Hilary hurries in, very excited)*

**Hilary:** Derek says ... oh, hi Joan.

**Joan:** *(Trying)* Hi Hilary.

| | |
|---|---|
| **Hilary:** | Derek says can you put the big lights on outside? |
| **Vinny:** | The security ones? |
| **Hilary:** | Yes, so we can see them better. |
| **Vinny:** | Certainly Hilary. |
| **Hilary:** | We think we saw the Doberman. |
| **Vinny:** | Oh good. |
| **Hilary:** | This is really exciting. |

*(She goes. Vinny turns on the outside white light from the Remote Control)*

| | |
|---|---|
| **Joan:** | If you turn that on ... |
| **Vinny:** | Never mind that – you go this minute and get on to Prentice. |
| **Joan:** | But my ma says if he only comes for a drink ... |
| **Vinny:** | Never mind your ma – he's coming for nothing – he should never have been invited in the first place – because they are right: he's the weirdest, most twisted pervert on this estate ... and you dressed like that. |
| **Joan:** | Like what ...? |
| **Vinny:** | And they don't like him and I don't want him coming in here ruining everything just when everything is going great ... |
| **Joan:** | But if he only comes for a drink ... |
| **Derek:** | *(Off)* Vinny? Vinny? |
| **Vinny:** | *(Calls)* Yes, Derek? |

*(Derek comes in, very excited)*

| | |
|---|---|
| **Derek:** | Vinny, they seem to ... oh hi Joan. |
| **Joan:** | *(Trying)* Hi Derek. |
| **Derek:** | They seem to have run from the lights. |
| **Vinny:** | Ah yes, probably at the side of the house. |
| **Derek:** | *(Indicates)* Yes, around there ... |
| **Vinny:** | Tell you what: go into the morning room, first door on your right ... |
| **Derek:** | Left of your hall-door? |
| **Vinny:** | Yes, the bay window there overlooks the side of the house ... |
| **Derek:** | Excellent – and we won't turn on the lights. |
| **Vinny:** | No, don't. |

**Derek:**  I'm enjoying this, Vinny.

**Vinny:**  Knew you would, Derek.

**Derek:**  Only wish Amanda and Tony were here – and maybe Colm O'Reilly as well.

**Vinny:**  We'll have them next time, Derek.

*(He goes excitedly. Vinny turns to Joan)*

**Vinny:**  I want no arguments, Joan, from you or your mother – that pervert's not to come here for a drink or for anything and that's that. And while we're on the subject of perverts, what's all this about you wanting him to look at you having a baby?

**Joan:**  Mr Prentice?

**Vinny:**  Him! Derek! He said you said you'd be delighted if he was there looking at you having a baby.

**Joan:**  That was because you told me to be agreeable.

**Vinny:**  Jesus Christ, not *that* agreeable.

**Joan:**  *(Angrily)* Anyway, I'm not going to have one, am I?

**Vinny:**  I'm not talking about whether you ...

**Joan:**  *(Suddenly furious)* No, you never want to talk about it, do you – that's your whole trouble.

**Vinny:**  Don't start that now!

**Joan:**  You just want to go on thinking it's all my fault ...

**Vinny:**  Joan ...

**Joan:**  I'm no good at cooking, no good at inviting people, no good at contributing and no good at having babies ...

**Vinny:**  For God's sake ...

**Joan:**  Well you may as well know that my ma thinks that it isn't my fault at all.

**Vinny:**  Nobody said ...

**Joan:**  She thinks you're the one to blame.

**Vinny:**  Me?

**Joan:**  Well you're the one that won't go to the doctor.

**Vinny:**  There's no need for me ...

**Joan:**  I went.

**Vinny:**  You wanted to go ...

**Joan:**   And she says you won't go because you're afraid what they'll find when they check your sperm-count.

**Vinny:**   What the hell are you talking about – there's nothing wrong with my sperm-count.

**Joan:**   Then why don't you have it checked?

**Vinny:**   There's nothing to check.

**Joan:**   Then why have all my sisters got babies?

**Vinny:**   How the hell do I ...

**Joan:**   Well my ma says it's because they're not married to you!

**Vinny:**   *(Furious)* Oh I see – great – grand. Well now that you've got that off your chest, maybe you'll do something useful – and phone your pervert friend Prentice and tell him not to appear next or near this house ...

**Joan:**   I'll be delighted to – because I hate this bloody house and this bloody estate and you for dragging me into it – Mr Fix-It!
           *(Derek and Hilary come in, very happy and excited. Vinny will turn the outside lights back to blue)*

**Derek:**   They really are running wild now – hi Joan.
           *(Joan runs angrily back to the kitchen)*

**Hilary:**   Is Joan all right?

**Vinny:**   Joan? Yes – she's just gone to get you some water.

**Hilary:**   Oh, the perfect hostess.

**Derek:**   They are absolutely ferocious – we thought they were savaging something ... or each other.

**Vinny:**   Yes, I think they've had their fun now.
           *(Vinny whistles. The dogs stop. Silence)*

**Derek:**   What happened? They've stopped.

**Hilary:**   Vinny whistled, didn't you?

**Vinny:**   *(Proudly)* That's all it takes.

**Derek:**   But how did they hear you?

**Hilary:**   Is it a sound only dogs can hear?

**Vinny:**   You heard me – and they must have heard me ...

**Derek:**   That's fantastic ...

**Vinny:**   It's all about control, Derek. It would now be

perfectly safe to walk anywhere in that garden.

**Derek:**  I'll take your word for that!

**Hilary:**  *(Listening)* Not even a whimper.

**Vinny:**  No, seriously, Derek, you could. Open the window there and see if you can see them.

**Derek:**  Open the window?!

**Vinny:**  Just look out – see if they're there.

**Derek:**  *(Laughs)* With all due respects, Vinny – I will in my arse.

**Hilary:**  Derek!

**Derek:**  *(Laughs)* A Doberman, an Alsatian and a Rottweiler?
*(Vinny whistles)*

**Vinny:**  Now. They'll be nowhere near the window.

**Derek:**  Ha-ha.

**Vinny:**  And even if they were, they won't come near you. It's perfectly safe, Derek – trust me.

**Derek:**  Are you serious?

**Vinny:**  Derek, security and guard-dog control is my business.

**Derek:**  Hilary?

**Hilary:**  *I* would not do it.

**Vinny:**  It's perfectly safe, Hilary.

**Derek:**  *(Bravely)* Okay then, never let it be said.

**Hilary:**  *(Nervously)* Are you sure, Vinny?

**Vinny:**  This is my profession.

**Derek:**  Give my love to Simon and Rebecca.

**Hilary:**  And me?

**Derek:**  Of course, darling.
*(Derek goes to the window. Peeps nervously out through the slits of the blinds. The phones suddenly tinkle)*

**Derek:**  *(Jumps back)* What's that?!

**Vinny:**  That's nothing – just Joan telling Prentice not to come.

**Derek:**  I'd prefer to deal with Prentice than with these boyos.

**Vinny:**  You're okay. Just let up the blind and the window

|            | opens upwards. |
|------------|---------------|
| **Derek:** | Right. *(Turns back to Vinny. Nervously).* And you're sure about this? |
| **Vinny:** | Couldn't be more sure. |
|            | *(Derek has raised the blind. He now very cautiously opens the window up and tentatively bends down and puts his head out)* |
| **Hilary:** | Can you see them, darling? |
| **Derek:** | *(Braver now)* No. Difficult to see in this light. *(Leans out and down more)* Very dark down here. |
| **Vinny:** | Can you hear anything? |
| **Derek:** | Don't think so. No sign of anything. Maybe they're asleep or something. Wait now ... I think I ... |
| **Hilary:** | Be careful – don't fall ... |
| **Derek:** | Just lean out a bit more. .. |
|            | *(Suddenly the dogs start again – close to Derek, louder than before with the window open – very savage)* |
| **Derek:** | *(Roars)* Jesus Christ! |
|            | *(He pulls his head in, bangs it against the window, stumbles, falls back in total panic)* |
| **Hilary:** | *(Shouts)* Derek! Are you all right? |
| **Derek:** | *(Holds his face)* They got me! They got me! |
| **Hilary:** | *(Afraid to move. Screams)* Derek! |
| **Vinny:** | *(Anxiously)* It's all right! |
| **Derek:** | *(To Hilary)* Close the window! |
| **Hilary:** | *(Afraid. To Vinny)* Vinny! |
| **Derek:** | *(Furious)* Hilary, close the shaggin' window! |
| **Hilary:** | Vinny! |
| **Vinny:** | *(Shouts)* Listen, listen – it's all right! |
| **Derek:** | *(Shouts at Hilary)* Close it, you stupid bitch! |
| **Vinny:** | *(Shouts)* I'm closing it! |
|            | *(Vinny runs to the window, collides with Derek struggling to his feet, still holding his face. Vinny falls)* |
| **Derek:** | *(To Hilary)* What are you doing standing there? |
| **Hilary:** | *(Terrified)* The dogs are outside! |
| **Derek:** | You were always bloody useless! |

*(Vinny has closed the window. The dogs still barking savagely)*

**Vinny:** Stop! Please stop! It's all right!

**Derek:** *(To Vinny)* Those shaggin' things should be destroyed.

**Vinny:** No, there's no need ...

**Derek:** There's every shaggin' need and I'm reporting them!

**Hilary:** *(Shouts at Vinny)* Our car is out there.

**Derek:** *(Shouts at Hilary)* Is that all you can think of – our car?!

**Hilary:** *(Shouts at Derek)* Don't you shout at me!

**Derek:** All money and no brains – A Rich Bitch – that's all you ever were!

**Hilary:** *(Furiously)* You were very glad of our money to get where you are!
*(Vinny has been furiously fumbling a small remote control from his pocket. He has now managed to press the correct buttons. All sounds suddenly stop – as we hear:)*

**Derek:** I never needed your shaggin' money!
*(Derek and Hilary stop, realising the silence)*

**Vinny:** Please – everything is all right ... when you have this.

**Derek:** What happened?

**Vinny:** Miniature remote control – pocket size – switches the dogs on and off.

**Derek:** You mean it's all on a tape recording ...?

**Vinny:** *(Proudly)* Yes! All at the press of a button – that way you have all the advantages of your guard dog: protection, comfort, deterrent to unwanted intruders – without any of the disadvantages: dog licences, dog food, dog dirt on your shoes late at night.

**Hilary:** So there are no dogs there at all?

**Derek:** *(Still annoyed)* No – it's all on a tape.

**Vinny:** Activated by your concealed control here and relayed through strategically positioned speakers in

|  |  |
|---|---|
| | your garden. One speaker is right under that window. |
| **Hilary:** | Then why did you whistle ... why did you turn off the outside alarm ...? |
| **Derek:** | *(Annoyed with her)* That was only an act ... |
| **Vinny:** | Just a little trick to put you off the scent, for the demonstration. Put the alarms back on now ... *(Throws the wall switch. To Derek)* You didn't hurt yourself or anything? |
| **Derek:** | No no, I'm fine. *(Now going with it)* And that is really very good, Vinny – really clever. |
| **Hilary:** | You hit your head – you must have hurt it. |
| **Derek:** | *(Annoyed)* It's fine. *(To Vinny)* What I liked was the authentic sound. |
| **Vinny:** | The sound is a vital component, Derek. |
| **Hilary:** | But you must have hurt it – you shouted. |
| **Derek:** | *(Sharply)* I said I'm fine. |
| **Hilary:** | But if you shouted you must have ... |
| **Derek:** | Hilary, will you shut-up about it – if I say I'm fine, I'm fine. |
| **Hilary:** | *(Sharply)* Oh sorry, I forgot – you're a doctor. |
| **Derek:** | Meaning what? |
| **Hilary:** | And I haven't forgotten what you called me – and don't think I have. |
| **Derek:** | *(To Vinny)* As I was saying, Vinny, I like that very much indeed. |
| **Vinny:** | It's very popular – one of our big sellers simply because people are completely fooled by it. |
| **Derek:** | Yes, I can see that – though I had my suspicions: the way they suddenly stopped and started again is a give-away. |
| **Hilary:** | You obviously thought they were real if you ... |
| **Derek:** | *(Sharply)* I'm not saying I didn't think they were real – I'm saying I had my suspicions. |
| **Vinny:** | Though your average burglar wouldn't have time to work that out. |
| **Derek:** | Which is the whole point. |
| **Vinny:** | Exactly – and surveys show that your top burglar |

deterrent is not, as you might think, your burglar alarm – but your barking dog.

**Derek:** I always said that – and yet how many burglar alarms do you see all over Sycamore Estate?

**Vinny:** Exactly and what people don't know is that burglars laugh at them: your average burglar knows he has exactly four minutes to do whatever he wants to do and go. They are, in effect, useless.

**Derek:** Well, it stands to reason.

**Hilary:** *(Still annoyed at Derek)* But *we* have a burglar alarm.

**Derek:** *(Still annoyed at her)* Hilary, we all have burglar alarms for the house insurance but I personally never had any faith in them. Never.

**Hilary:** *(Sweetly)* Well isn't that nice to know, Vinny – and the children and I left in the house all day.

**Derek:** *(Sweetly)* Except she's never *in* the house.

**Hilary:** Oh I wonder where I am then.

**Derek:** *(Equally sweetly)* I'll tell you exactly where you are – you're out at your keep-fit classes or your coffee mornings or you're ferrying the children to the pre-school in the winter or to the beach in the summer – you are lots of places, Hilary, but in the house you are not.

**Hilary:** I wonder who does all the cooking and cleaning then – or maybe it's all done in four minutes by your average burglar while our useless alarm bell is ringing!

*(An angry silence. Vinny uneasy. Then Joan enters)*

**Joan:** *(Tentatively)* Vinny ....?

**Vinny:** Ah Joan, have you got Hilary's water?

**Joan:** No – but them things have arrived.

**Vinny:** What things?

**Joan:** They were delivered at the back door. So I'll go ahead, will I?

**Vinny:** *(Quickly)* Oh right – do – and get Hilary's water. *(Vinny anxiously ushers Joan out. The silence still* *very angry)*

**Vinny:**   Would you like to hear some more ... before dinner?

**Derek:**   More what, Vinny?

**Vinny:**   Sounds.

**Derek:**   Of more barking dogs, you mean?

**Vinny:**   No – sounds for relaxation.

**Derek:**   *(Coldly)* Yes, great idea – I'm all for relaxation.

**Vinny:**   I think you'll enjoy these ... *(Begins to programme his remote control)*

**Derek:**   Don't mind if I ...? *(Towards the drinks)*

**Vinny:**   No no, fire away. *(To Hilary)* Joan will be out with your water as soon as ...

**Hilary:**   *(Annoyed)* I can wait.

**Vinny:**   Probably has the tap running, getting it nice and cold.

           *(The phones tinkle – Joan making another phone-call)*

**Vinny:**   *(Quietly, to the phone)* Christ! *(To Hilary)* Or you wouldn't prefer to switch to a sherry, would you?

**Hilary:**   *(Coldly)* No, I'd prefer to wait for the water.

**Vinny:**   I can get you a sherry here ...

**Hilary:**   No, thank you – I'd hate to be responsible for draining the reservoir for nothing.

**Vinny:**   *(Bravely)* Sure. Well now, here we go. Dim the lights for this ... then I think Joan will be serving dinner. *(Vinny has taken the remote control. Presses a button. The lights dim to a gentle glow. Proudly)* Now supposing Joan and me are sitting here, just relaxing or whatever, and we want to get that cosy feeling ... *(Presses a button. There is a very gentle sound of rain on the roof)* and you get rain on the roof ... or you may want it a little heavier maybe ... *(Presses a button: the rain is heavier)* to feel even cosier...

**Derek:**   *(Impressed)* That is good.

**Hilary:**   *(Reluctantly impressed)* Yes.

**Derek:**   Very good indeed.

**Vinny:**   Or, if you want to get that really cosy feeling of being in out of the storm when everyone else is getting soaked ... (*Presses a button. Now it turns into a storm – wind, thunder, rain*)

**Hilary:** (*Impressed*) Fantastic.

**Vinny:** Or you might want to be away from it all, down on a farm, on your holidays, in the early morning ... (*Presses a button: bird-song, low cow sounds and then sound of cock-crow*)

**Hilary:** Lovely.

**Derek:** (*Laughs*) Will it lay an egg for your breakfast as well?

**Vinny:** (*Joining in*) You never know, Derek. Or is that an aeroplane I see coming into view or is it a jet plane ... (*Presses a button: a jet plane comes in quickly, screams through the room and rumbles away*)

**Derek:** (*Enjoying this*) Duck!

**Vinny:** Or maybe Joan and I want to be off on a cruise (*A ship's horn is heard, seagulls, waves against the bow*) ... or have we landed on a desert island – this is Joan's favourite (*The sound of waves on the shore and Hawaiian music*) ... or, sometimes, very late at night, she likes to sit down, dream a little, and hear this ... (*Vinny presses a button. The sound of a baby crying. Vinny immediately and anxiously tries to stop it. It goes on*) ... No ... that's ... that's just ... that's just a joke ... (*It stops*) This is the late night one ... (*The sound of an owl*) the wise old owl at the end of the day.

**Derek:** Great 'oul sound, eh? Get it? (*Laughs*)
(*Hilary has now warmed a little*)

**Hilary:** It is all so realistic.

**Vinny:** (*Proudly*) It means you never need to go out.

**Derek:** Absolutely.

**Vinny:** And the choice is endless: down by the sea, up the mountains, steam trains, authentic dance music ...
(*Vinny turns the lights up again*)

**Derek:** (*Now trying to make up*) That might be good to

have, Hilary.

**Vinny:** It's marketed as 'The Mood Maker' – and I personally think it will be a huge seller eventually.

**Derek:** *(To Hilary)* What do you think – have a few people in, turn it on – very impressive.

**Hilary:** That might be nice.

**Derek:** You haven't sold any others in the estate, have you? – Amanda and Tony, Georgina and Peter ...?

**Vinny:** No, you'd be the first – well, the second. It's not really security, but we like it.

**Derek:** I think we should talk about that, Vinny. And I'd be interested in those dogs too ... and maybe something for the club as well.

**Hilary:** *(Lightly)* Derek, we are here to enjoy ourselves.

**Derek:** *(Pleasantly)* 'Course we are, darling – not another word about business. *(To Vinny)* Brochure and estimate soon as you can.

**Vinny:** *(Joining in)* Have it in your letter-box first thing tomorrow.

**Derek:** Guaranteed?

**Vinny:** Absolutely. *(To Hilary)* There we are, Hilary – from now on, an enjoyable evening without a mention of business – guaranteed.

**Hilary:** *(Pleasantly)* You're as bad as he is.

*(Vinny and Derek enjoy this as Joan comes in. She carries a glass of water and seems very assured)*

**Vinny:** Ah Joan. Welcome.

**Joan:** *(To Hilary)* I had the tap running.

**Vinny:** I said you'd be doing that.

**Derek:** *(Merrily)* It must be exhausted by now – running! *(Laughter)*

**Hilary:** Don't mind him – thank you so much, Joan.

**Vinny:** *(Hopefully)* And everything else ready or ...?

**Joan:** Yes, everything is ready – Tuna pizzas for Derek and Hilary, Ham and Pineapple pizzas for us with coleslaw, garlic bread and a side-salad of lettuce and scallions, followed by fresh fruit salad for dessert, followed by coffee and the After-

|          | Eights. |
|----------|---------|
| **Derek:** | My stomach says 'great' ... |
| **Hilary:** | Wonderful – and worth waiting for. |
| **Joan:** | And we think, as it's pizzas, if we had it on our laps in the television room ... *(To Vinny)* my ma says in case we want to watch ... |
| **Vinny:** | *(Quickly)* Excellent – *(To Hilary)* Now, isn't this the enjoyment I promised you? |
| **Hilary:** | Indeed it is ... |
| **Derek:** | And the food you promised – thank you, Joan. |
| **Vinny:** | We always keep our promises – so maybe you'd take your drinks if you'd like to follow me ... |
| **Derek:** | Yes, gladly, I think ... |
| **Vinny:** | You can bring in the food, Joan – and maybe Derek's bottle of wine ... |
| **Joan:** | *(Happily)* Oh right, I will. |
|          | *(As Joan turns towards the kitchen and Vinny merrily leads Hilary and Derek to the door, the red-alarm light suddenly flashes and its bleep is heard)* |
| **Vinny:** | Who could that be? |
| **Hilary:** | Is it your door? |
| **Derek:** | It's your alarm, isn't it? |
| **Vinny:** | Yes, but we're not expecting anyone. *(Turns it off)* |
| **Joan:** | Oh God! |
| **Hilary:** | What is it, Joan? |
| **Joan:** | Oh Vinny, I'm terrible sorry – with taking in the stuff and getting the dinner and listening to me ma ... |
| **Vinny:** | You didn't forget ...? |
| **Joan:** | I forgot to ring Mr Prentice. |
| **Derek:** | You don't mean that's him now, do you? |
| **Joan:** | Vinny, I'm terrible sorry ... |
| **Vinny:** | The one thing we asked you to do! |
| **Hilary:** | Oh what matter. |
| **Derek:** | What matter! He's a freak, an upstart and he's out to ruin you, me, everyone on this estate – and I made myself perfectly clear ... |
| **Vinny:** | It's all right, Derek, listen ... it might not be him at |

all ...

**Derek:**    But you're not expecting anyone else...

**Hilary:**    It could be some neighbours – Amanda and Tony maybe?

**Vinny:**    Could be – but this security monitor will show us, at the touch of a button who it is ... and as it's not nine o'clock yet, I'd be personally surprised if it is him ...

*(The wall-panel automatically reveals the monitor. All look to see the face of Prentice, large, close and threatening, staring out from the screen ... as the door-bell rings melodiously)*

**Derek:**    *(Accusing)* And who's that?

**Joan:**    Oh God, Vinny, I'm terrible sorry ...

**Vinny:**    *(Angrily to Joan)* Joan, how could you do this to me!

**Derek:**    After all I said, he's here!

*(The door-bell rings again as Joan, Hilary, Derek and Vinny look at the screen. We fade to darkness, leaving only the face of Prentice staring out from the screen. Hold. Then it too fades)*

*END OF ACT ONE*

# ACT TWO

*Seconds later.*

*In the darkness, only the monitor is illuminated with Prentice's face as before – large and threatening. Now lights. Vinny, Derek, Hilary and Joan, watching the monitor, in a freeze. Immediately, the door-bell rings again, bringing all to life.*

**Derek:** *(To Vinny)* But I thought you said he had been phoned ...

**Joan:** It's all my fault – I forgot all about it because I was getting the dinner ...

**Hilary:** Oh, what matter ...?

**Joan:** ... and now it'll be getting cold.

**Derek:** I'd never have come if I thought he was coming ...

**Vinny:** *(Louder)* Listen everybody, listen: I think I have the solution and there's no need for any panic – because what we can do now is let him in ...
*(The door-bell rings again)*

**Derek:** Not much choice in that ...

**Vinny:** ... and then I can tell him that you've all just arrived a few seconds ago and ... and ... that you're all only here for one drink, and we needn't mention a word about dinner to him at all ... *(Turns off the monitor)*

**Derek:** *(Liking this)* Right – and if we say we haven't even had our drink yet ...

**Vinny:** ... then it'll look as if we're all only starting – we'll get rid of the glasses – *then* we all have our one drink, with him, while we chat about whatever we like ...

**Derek:** This is good.

**Joan:** But the dinner will be getting cold ...

**Vinny:** *(Sharply)* Put it in the oven!

**Joan:** But there's lettuce!

**Vinny:** *(Decides to ignore this. To Derek)* Then after we

have our one drink, we'll make sure he goes first
and, once he's gone, then we sit down and have
our dinner and our chat as planned, as if he never
arrived.

**Hilary:** But what harm if he stays longer ...?

**Vinny:** No, Hilary, we all made a mistake – myself as
well as Joan – but we can still correct it.

**Derek:** Vinny's right – and the sooner we let him in, the
sooner he'll be gone ...

**Vinny:** Exactly ...

**Derek:** Because to tell you the truth, I am absolutely ravenous.

*(The bell rings again)*

**Vinny:** Ten minutes, Derek, maximum, and he'll be away
– guaranteed. And Joan, maybe you'd put on
some music ...

**Joan:** Vinny, the pizzas will be ...

**Vinny:** *(Angrily)* ... and then put the pizzas in the oven,
lettuce on a plate.

**Derek:** Like your style, Vinny – I always say 'it's not the
mistakes we make, but how we correct them!'

**Vinny:** Let you in on a secret, Derek – before I went out
on my own, I was known to everybody as Mr Fix-
It. Crisis? – call in Vinny.

**Derek:** I believe it.

**Vinny:** Music, Joan, then the oven.

*(Vinny goes. Derek collects the glasses as Joan gets the
remote control)*

**Hilary:** Behave yourself now, Derek.

**Derek:** Oh I will. In fact, I may take the opportunity to
ask our friend some pertinent questions.

**Joan:** Is there something you'd like to hear?

**Hilary:** What was on was lovely, Joan.

**Joan:** Right. *(Tries pressing some buttons nothing happens.
Panic)* Oh God!

**Derek:** Want a hand with that, Joan?

**Joan:** *(Struggling)* No, I think I can manage it.

**Derek:** Just press 3 and 5 together and point it at the

stereo ...

**Hilary:** She can manage it.

**Derek:** I'm not saying she can't manage it!

**Joan:** *(Struggling)* Oh God help me ... oh come on!

*(Joan presses some buttons. Gets it wrong. All hell seems to break loose. She cries out as: A crack of thunder is heard, a jet screams through, the lights dance and the music comes on at high speed. A red light hits the door as Vinny hurries in, closing the door behind him. He rushes to Joan as she struggles to correct)*

**Vinny:** For God's sake!

**Joan:** I was only trying to ...

**Derek:** You should have let me do it, Joan ...

**Vinny:** You should have let Derek do it.

**Hilary:** Derek should have left her alone to do it.

*(Vinny has corrected all. Sounds end, lights normal – but the music still fast)*

**Vinny:** There we are.

**Joan:** The music is still going wrong.

**Vinny:** *(Furious)* Wrongly! – get something right, will you?!

*(Joan runs quickly to the kitchen as Vinny adjusts the music)*

**Vinny:** Now. *(Calmly to Derek)* Everything okay here?

**Derek:** All ready.

**Hilary:** Is Joan all right?

**Vinny:** Oh yes – just looking in at the dinner ... but say nothing because you've just arrived. *(Opens the door)* Come in, Mr Prentice.

*(Prentice is 60, polite and quiet, dressed in his best sports-jacket. He wears glasses. His accent is local to the area. He peeps in cautiously before entering)*

**Prentice:** Everything all right?

**Vinny:** Everything's grand – that's part of our security system. Now, everyone, this is Mr Prentice, just dropped in for one drink, same as yourselves. *(To Prentice)* This is Derek Maguire, just arrived before you ...

**Prentice:** *(Offers his hand)* Good evening, sir.

**Derek:** *(Coldly)* 'Evening.

**Vinny:** And Derek's wife, Hilary.

**Hilary:** *(Shakes hands)* Pleased to meet you.

**Prentice:** Pleased to meet you.

**Vinny:** Derek and Hilary live up in Sycamore Grove – the detached open-plan bungalows with the double garages.

**Prentice:** Oh, grand houses.

**Hilary:** *(Kindly)* And you're in the old house?

**Prentice:** I am, I am.

**Hilary:** With the big Sycamore tree?

**Prentice:** That's the one.

**Derek:** *(Coldly)* That you wanted chopped down.

**Prentice:** Pardon me?

**Derek:** The only sycamore tree in Sycamore Estate and you wanted to chop it down.

**Prentice:** Well, you see, it's on my land ...

**Derek:** But you were stopped by our Residents' Association.

**Prentice:** *(Friendly)* I was, I was. It's still there.

**Derek:** *(Triumph)* It is indeed – and there it will stay.
*(The phones tinkle – Joan dialling out)*

**Vinny:** *(To the phones)* God! *(Now anxiously to all)* Right – well sit down everybody – my wife is also here – she is in the kitchen, back any minute.

**Prentice:** Grand.
*(Prentice has innocently chosen the chair where Derek has been sitting. Derek chooses another, as Vinny watches, helplessly)*

**Vinny:** Okay – so now that we're all here, we'll have that drink ...

**Derek:** Bushmills for me – then we'll be off.

**Vinny:** Fine, Derek. Hilary?

**Hilary:** Glass of water.

**Vinny:** Water – great. Mr Prentice?

**Prentice:** A bottle of Guinness would be grand.

**Vinny:** Yes, I think we have Guinness in the fridge. *(Going)* I'll tell Joan while she's getting your water, Hilary.

**Hilary:** *(Stands)* Or will I ...?

**Vinny:** No no – and maybe you'd look after a Bushmills for me too, Derek?

**Derek:** *(On his feet)* Will do, Vin.

**Vinny:** Thanks, Der. *(Presses the intercom button)* Come in, kitchen, come in please. Over.

**Joan:** *(v/o grumpily)* What?

**Vinny:** Pardon. Lounge here, kitchen – a bottle of Guinness for Mr Prentice while you're getting a glass of water for Hilary.

**Joan:** *(v/o)* Right.

**Vinny:** Many thanks – soon as you can – over and out. *(Switches off)*

**Derek:** Hey, I like that.

**Vinny:** The inter-room intercom? Yes, we find it invaluable when entertaining.

**Derek:** I'd say.

**Vinny:** But more important, on a security level it gives us, at the press of a button, the facility to contact any room in the house, including the bathrooms. Could be a life-saver in a security crisis.

**Derek:** Indeed. *(Confidentially)* Maybe we can talk about that too – anon?

**Vinny:** No problem, Derek – ten-year guarantee, including parts and labour. *(Takes his drink)* Ta.

**Derek:** Cheers.
*(Awkward silence)*

**Hilary:** Do you have burglar alarms and things, Mr Prentice?

**Prentice:** Ah, I never had much time for them – living on my own and that.

**Vinny:** Living on your own is the best reason for having security.

**Derek:** Precisely.

**Prentice:** I never bothered much with anything beyond a

|  | good lock. |
|---|---|
| **Vinny:** | *(Amused)* Mr Prentice, the days of depending on a good lock are gone. |
| **Derek:** | Absolutely. |
| **Vinny:** | *(Authoritatively)* What you should have, minimum, are security dead-locks on all doors and windows, a reliable burglar alarm and a good guard-dog. |
| **Derek:** | *(Private joke)* Like your's, Vinny. |
| **Vinny:** | Exactly – or, maximum, you could go for something as sophisticated as you see here – monitors, inter-room intercoms, sensor alarms in house and garden. |
| **Prentice:** | Ah, I don't think so. |
| **Vinny:** | *(Challenging)* You don't think what – that you shouldn't have all this or you shouldn't have the alarms and the guard-dog? |
| **Prentice:** | I never bothered with anything beyond a good lock. |
| **Vinny:** | *(Amused)* So you're saying I'm wrong – that all my advice about security is irrelevant? |
| **Prentice:** | Well I never bothered with anything beyond a good lock. |
| **Vinny:** | *(Controlled)* So what you're saying is ...? |
| **Derek:** | Allow me, Vinny. *(Then)* Mr Prentice, what is your business? |
| **Prentice:** | Pardon me? |
| **Derek:** | What do you do – what is your line of expertise? |
| **Prentice:** | I'm a retired farmer. |
| **Derek:** | So you know all about farming: that's your business, that's your line of expertise and we wouldn't pretend to know as much about farming as you do. Now, Vinny is a security engineer – that's his business, that's his line of expertise ... |
| **Prentice:** | *(Kindly)* And wouldn't you know it, with all these marvellous gadgets... |
| **Derek:** | Precisely. Now if ... |
| **Prentice:** | *(To Vinny)* I knew you'd be a security engineer. |

**Derek:**    And he is – and you're a farmer ...
**Prentice:** A retired farmer ...
**Derek:**    *(Patiently)* A retired farmer. Now my point is ...
**Hilary:**   Mr Prentice, would you like to guess what Derek is?
**Derek:**    Hilary, that has nothing to do with anything.
**Hilary:**   But it would be interesting ...
**Derek:**    *(Angrily)* Except that is it not what we are talking about!
**Hilary:**   I just think it would be interesting to hear ...
**Prentice:** *(Looks)* He does advertising, doesn't he?
**Hilary:**   *(Stops. To Derek)* How did he know that?
**Derek:**    Hilary, as it's my job, he just might know it.
**Hilary:**   But everyone says you look like a doctor.
**Derek:**    They don't!
**Hilary:**   Darling, they do.
**Derek:**    They obviously don't.
**Hilary:**   Well Vinny did.
**Vinny:**    Yes, I did – and you definitely do.
**Derek:**    All right – Vinny did.
**Hilary:**   And Joan did.
**Derek:**    *(Barely controlled)* All right – and Joan did but he *(Prentice)* didn't, did he? – so I don't.
**Prentice:** Look like a doctor, is it?
**Hilary:**   Yes, don't you think he looks like a doctor?
**Derek:**    He's already said ...
**Prentice:** Oh you do, sir – I'd've thought that.
**Derek:**    You obviously didn't think it!
**Prentice:** But I would, only it was in the papers that you were doing the advertising.
**Derek:**    What papers?
**Prentice:** In the papers it said Mr Colm O'Reilly was asking you to do the advertising for the extension, up beyond the New Road.
**Derek:**    That was never in the papers.
**Hilary:**   It must have been, darling, if he knows you're not a doctor.
**Derek:**    It wasn't! It's still to be confirmed between the

|                |                                                                      |
| -------------- | -------------------------------------------------------------------- |
|                | developer and Colm O'Reilly.                                         |
| **Prentice:**  | Only for that I would have said you were a doctor.                   |
| **Hilary:**    | There!                                                               |
| **Prentice:**  | Because I think you look very like one.                             |
| **Hilary:**    | Exactly – everyone does.                                            |
| **Derek:**     | For God's sake!                                                     |

**Prentice:** (*To Hilary*) To tell you the truth, he doesn't look like a man that does advertising at all.

**Hilary:** I know – but do you know (*sings*) 'The Commodore bed is the bed to rely on'?

**Derek:** Hilary!

**Hilary:** No, he might know it. (*To Prentice*) It's the ad on the television.

**Prentice:** I don't have a television.

**Vinny:** It's also on the buses.

**Hilary:** And in selected railway stations.

**Derek:** Listen – we're not discussing the Commodore bed – and he obviously knows nothing about it anyway.

**Prentice:** Is it the one with the polar bears?

**Hilary:** Yes! He knows it, Derek.

**Derek:** So he knows it – but all of this is not the point. The point is that your line of expertise is farming, mine is advertising ...

**Hilary:** Although you do look like a doctor and your first love would always be ...

**Derek:** (*Furious*) Shut-up Hilary! – and Vinny's is security and if he says you should have security, then you should have it. That is, and always was, the point – if I was allowed to make it!

**Hilary:** (*Angrily*) And now you've made it – Congratulations.

(*Angry silence*)

**Prentice:** (*Repentant*) Or maybe I just *heard* that you were in advertising – my whole trouble is that I talk to everyone.

**Derek:** (*Quietly*) When you're not smearing cars with

manure or peeping in windows.

**Vinny:** *(Awkwardly)* My point was simply that, these days, every house needs good security.

**Prentice:** *(Kindly)* And you're probably right, sir – because my other trouble is that I remember all this place when it was only fields – beyond there was Sheridan's Farm, Gallagher's Gully ran down the back here and all along the road outside was Daisy Hill and that's where myself and my mother would bring the cattle down and, in the summer, you'd hardly see the grass for the daisies – that's where it got its name and it's still called that by some of the farmers that worked here ...

**Hilary:** Really?

**Prentice:** Oh yes – and in them days my poor mother hardly locked the door at night, never mind have an alarm.

**Vinny:** *(Hard)* And our point, Mr Prentice, is those days are gone.

**Prentice:** They are – so maybe I will get a bit of security and maybe I'll get it from yourself.

**Derek:** *(Hard)* Do. *(Quietly to Vinny)* Any sign of his Guinness?

**Vinny:** *(Quietly)* Any minute now – you might like to look at the house's security while he's having it.

**Derek:** *(Quietly)* Good idea.

**Vinny:** *(Quietly)* Soon as it arrives, we'll leave them to it.

**Hilary:** Do you still live with your mother, Mr Prentice?

**Prentice:** Ah no – she died eight years ago.

**Hilary:** Oh dear.

**Prentice:** You mentioned the Sycamore tree beside my house.

**Hilary:** Oh yes, I think it is really beautiful.

**Derek:** We all do. *(A point)* Well, nearly all.

**Vinny:** The very first photos we took when we moved to Sycamore were of that tree.

**Hilary:** At last summer's Residents' Association Bar-B-Q, I shot some lovely video of the children climbing it ...

**Derek:** I filmed that, Hilary.

**Hilary:** No, darling, I did.

**Derek:** But you couldn't have – you're in it!

**Hilary:** All right, I may be in some of it, but you didn't film it because that day you had your First Aid examinations and arrived back with that big trophy ...

**Derek:** You're right – the Perpetual Cup.

**Hilary:** *(To Vinny)* We had to put some old ones *under* the cabinet to fit it in. But sorry, Mr Prentice, I interrupted you.

**Prentice:** No no, just that one morning, my mother dressed herself up in her Sunday best, had her breakfast, washed-up after, turned off the wireless, went out to that Sycamore tree and hanged herself.
*(Stunned silence)*

**Hilary:** I beg your pardon?

**Prentice:** I was off out taking in the carrots at the time so I didn't find her for nearly three hours.
*(Joan comes in, carrying a glass of water and a glass of Guinness)*

**Vinny:** *(Brightly)* Ah, here we are now.

**Joan:** I left the tap running.

**Vinny:** Great – well everything is grand here – you know Mr Prentice.

**Prentice:** *(To Joan)* Well well well, there we are now.

**Joan:** Hello Mr Prentice – how are you?

**Prentice:** Thinking of taking your husband's advice about security.

**Joan:** Oh yes, Vinny knows all about that. Guinness for you.

**Vinny:** *(Takes the water)* And the water for Hilary.

**Hilary:** *(Still stunned)* Many thanks, Joan.

**Joan:** Not at all. *(To Vinny)* It's in the oven.

**Vinny:** Great. Derek was saying he'd like to look at our security system here ...

**Derek:** *(Pointed)* Then we'll be off home.

**Joan:** Oh grand.

**Vinny:** We'll take our drinks with us.

**Joan:** Grand.

**Prentice:** *(To Joan)* And how's your mother, Mabel?
*(Vinny and Derek pause at hearing this)*

**Joan:** *(Easily)* Oh couldn't be better. I was just on to her now and she said to say she was asking for you.

**Prentice:** And I return the compliment.

**Joan:** *(Giggles)* She'll be thrilled.

**Prentice:** She's a lovely woman, Mabel.

**Vinny:** *(Comes back)* Excuse me – maybe you should explain to Mr Prentice that your mother's name is Betty.

**Prentice:** Oh thanks very much – but I'd never call her by her first name.

**Vinny:** But you're already calling her Mabel.

**Joan:** No, Vinny, that's me.

**Vinny:** What's you?

**Joan:** That's what Mr Prentice calls me – not my mother.

**Vinny:** But your name's Joan.

**Prentice:** Do you know, I'd prefer Mabel.

**Vinny:** Would you? Well unfortunately her name happens to be Joan!

**Joan:** It's all right, Vinny – he only calls me that because of where we live. Forty-four Sycamore.

**Prentice:** *(Quotes)* 'I'll go to Forty-four Sycamore, go knock-knock-knock on the big front door and say is Mabel coming out tonight.'

**Vinny:** You'll do what?

**Joan:** It's a song!

**Prentice:** Ah before all your time – Phil Harris used to sing it.

**Vinny:** Did he? Ever hear of this song, Derek?

**Derek:** Never – but none of this surprises me.

**Hilary:** I think I heard of it.

**Joan:** *(To Hilary)* Yes, it goes *(sings)* 'Now Mabel is the one that's cute, so don't take any substitute; be

|            | sure it's Mabel and you'll be all right'. |
|------------|---|
| **Prentice:** | Didn't she pick that up quick? |
| **Vinny:** | Quickly! Yes she did and now she can put it down again! |
| **Joan:** | But it's only ... |
| **Vinny:** | *(Angrily)* I mean it, Joan – your name is and always was, Joan. |
| **Hilary:** | Oh Vinny, I think Mabel is nice ... |
| **Derek:** | Stay out of it, Hilary. |
| **Vinny:** | It may be nice, but it's not her name. |
| **Hilary:** | It doesn't have to be. Derek used to call me Bubbles once. |
| **Derek:** | What? |
| **Hilary:** | Before we were married you always called me Bubbles. |
| **Derek:** | Don't talk rubbish. |
| **Hilary:** | I have it on all your Valentine cards. |
| **Derek:** | Well I don't call you it now and that is the point. |
| **Vinny:** | And the other point is you weren't married when Derek called you that ... |
| **Hilary:** | ... oh very true ... |
| **Vinny:** | But Joan is a married woman and she's married to me and I call her Joan so her name remains Joan and nothing else. |
| **Derek:** | Precisely. |
| **Vinny:** | Okay with you, Mr Prentice? |
| **Prentice:** | Grand. |
| **Vinny:** | Good. |
| **Derek:** | *(Then)* Vinny, might visit your loo before our little security tour? |
| **Vinny:** | Sure Derek – we've a choice of three: second door where you came in or top of the stairs facing you or one in our master bedroom ... |
| **Derek:** | *(Going)* Great. |
| **Vinny:** | Any difficulty, there's an inter-room intercom in all loos ... |
| **Derek:** | Perfect ... |
| **Vinny:** | In fact, you can call me on one, if you want to |

|  | check the system ... |
| **Derek:** | *(Waits)* Good idea ... |
| **Vinny:** | Just press the button, I'll hear the buzzer here and connect you up ... |
| **Derek:** | Will do. |
|  | *(Derek has gone. Vinny waits by the intercom)* |
| **Hilary:** | I was very sorry to hear about your mother, Mr Prentice. |
| **Prentice:** | Ah these things happen. |
| **Hilary:** | Did you know about that, Joan? |
| **Joan:** | You mean about how she died ...? |
| **Hilary:** | Yes, Mr Prentice was saying she ... |
| **Joan:** | Oh yes, at the Sycamore tree, I know. *(To Prentice)* It was awful. |
| **Prentice:** | You were always very kind about that, Mabel. |
| **Vinny:** | Joan! |
| **Prentice:** | Oh my apologies – Joan. |
| **Vinny:** | *(To Joan)* And how do you know about that anyway? |
| **Joan:** | Mr Prentice said it. |
| **Vinny:** | But you were out in the kitchen when he said it. |
| **Joan:** | No, on our walks he said it. |
| **Prentice:** | She's a great walker and even better talker. |
| **Joan:** | *(Merrily)* I am not! |
| **Vinny:** | You never told me you went for walks. |
| **Joan:** | They're not walks – it's just when I go out I might meet him and he'd tell me where all the old farming places were: Cooper's Field, Gallagher's Gully, Daisy Hill and he said there used to be lovely horses in Sullivan's field ... |
|  | *(The intercom buzzer sounds)* |
| **Vinny:** | *(Angrily)* Did he? Well this is very interesting I must say. *(Presses the intercom button)* Lounge, over. |
| **Derek:** | *(v/o)* Ah Vinny – just checking in. Over. |
| **Vinny:** | And I'm receiving you loud and clear, Derek. Which loo are you in? |
| **Derek:** | Right of the front door. |

**Vinny:** Ah yes, with the china-blue tiling?

**Derek:** Yes – I think Amanda and Tony have their's in pink ...

**Vinny:** Oh right, yes, they do – so, all set for our security tour?

**Derek:** Looking forward to it – and this is very impressive, Vin.

**Vinny:** It's only the beginning – and I'm on my way. Over and out, Der.
*(Vinny switches off)*

**Prentice:** Begob that's wonderful.

**Vinny:** *(Abruptly)* Yeah. Joan, I'm going to see Derek now and we have our drinks with us, so they'll be off as soon as we get back.

**Joan:** All right.

**Vinny:** Your water all right there, Hilary?

**Hilary:** Just finishing it, Vinny.

**Vinny:** Excellent. If you need me, Joan, buzz me on the inter-room intercom ...

**Joan:** Right.

**Vinny:** And don't touch the remote control
*(As Vinny goes, he secretly takes the Bushmills bottle with him. He closes the door. The atmosphere is suddenly very light)*

**Joan:** *(Merrily accusing. To Prentice)* Thanks very much – You and your 'Mabel'!

**Prentice:** I thought he knew I called you Mabel.

**Joan:** Are you joking me?!

**Hilary:** I think that's great.

**Joan:** I knew he'd hit the ceiling – I can't even tell him I eat Battenburg cake in case he thinks I'm getting fat.

**Hilary:** God, I love Battenburg.

**Joan:** My ma brings it to me and I hide it in a drawer upstairs and as soon as he goes off in the morning, out comes coffee with three spoons of sugar – and as much Battenburg as I can stuff into my gob.

| | |
|---|---|
| **Hilary:** | *(Enjoying this)* You're not serious? |
| **Joan:** | My ma says that someday he's going to double-back and find me choked to death on the lot. |
| **Hilary:** | That's like our grass – Derek thinks I do it front and back every three weeks ... |
| **Joan:** | And you don't ...? |
| **Hilary:** | I give seven quid to a lovely young chap, tell him to use our mower and leave the bags where Derek can put them away. |
| **Joan:** | You'd be mad to do it yourself. |
| **Hilary:** | My only worry is that someday our Simon is going to say: 'Look daddy, there's the man who cuts our grass'. |
| **Joan:** | *(Of Prentice)* The same as this fellow with his 'Mabel'. |
| **Prentice:** | It suits you better than Joan. |
| **Joan:** | Don't say that again to Vinny ... *(To Hilary)* But tell me – used Derek really call you Bubbles? |
| **Hilary:** | Oh yes – when I had my hair in tight curls. The other morning, for something better to do, I took out all these old photos and there I was, looking like a golly-wog. What Derek ever saw in me I'll never know. |
| **Joan:** | I sometimes wonder why Vinny ever married me. |
| **Hilary:** | Oh I know why Derek *married* me – two words – Baby Simon. |
| **Joan:** | You weren't ...? |
| **Hilary:** | I was actually engaged to this other guy, but one fling with Derek – I think it was the bubbles that went to my head. |
| **Joan:** | God, my ma would've killed me if that happened to me. Now she wants to kill me because it's not happening! |
| **Prentice:** | A grand woman. |
| **Joan:** | *(To Prentice)* Here, I'll get you another bottle of Guinness. |
| **Prentice:** | No, I was only to have the one. |
| **Joan:** | Sure who'll know ... *(Takes his glass)* |

**Hilary:**    (*Stands*) You're right! Mind if I switch to a sherry?

**Joan:**    Fire ahead. Tell you what – you must come over some morning for a feast of Battenburg.

**Hilary:**    I will – while my grass is being cut! (*Goes to the drinks*)

**Prentice:**    (*Anxious. To Joan*) I don't think I'll ...

**Joan:**    Don't you worry, Mr Prentice.
    (*Joan goes into the kitchen. Hilary has her sherry*)

**Hilary:**    (*Then*) Just like to say I'm honestly very sorry about your mother.

**Prentice:**    Oh much obliged.

**Hilary:**    Not knowing why, I'm sure, makes it very difficult ...

**Prentice:**    Aye – though I have my suspicions.

**Hilary:**    I'm sure.

**Prentice:**    In that it all happened only two days after she signed the land away.

**Hilary:**    The land?

**Prentice:**    Our two farms – signed them over for next-to-nothing. Ah, she never understood these things, what she was doing ...

**Hilary:**    Oh dear.

**Prentice:**    Knew nothing about Compulsory Purchase Orders or Land Re-Zonings or Section Fours – and before we knew it, the bulldozers were in. That'd be my suspicions anyway.

**Hilary:**    Well, I'm awfully sorry.

**Prentice:**    There we are. (*Then*) And I'm sorry for not saying your husband was a doctor.

**Hilary:**    Well you're right – he isn't really.

**Prentice:**    But he does look like one.

**Hilary:**    Everyone says that – and he is very good and how he practises: every Thursday, hail rain or shine.

**Prentice:**    So that's where he's going.

**Hilary:**    Sorry?

**Prentice:**    On my walks, I sometimes see him on Thursdays ...

**Hilary:**   Going to his First Aid meetings?
**Prentice:**   Yes. He'd know Patti Mooney then?
**Hilary:**   Who?
**Prentice:**   Patricia Mooney – she lives beyond in the council houses – she's in that too, I think: the First Aid.
**Hilary:**   Then I'm sure he knows her.
**Prentice:**   They owned a farm here once – in fact, where Sycamore Crescent is now. The locals still call that Mooney's Field.
**Hilary:**   Really?
         *(Joan hurries back with a glass of Guinness)*
**Joan:**   They're coming, they're coming!
**Hilary:**   Derek and Vinny? *(In panic, she knocks back her sherry)*
**Joan:**   Yes! Take this quick, Mr Prentice.
**Prentice:**   *(Anxiously)* No – I won't have time ...
**Joan:**   Take it – they'll think it's your first.
**Hilary:**   Where are they?
**Joan:**   Out the back, examining everything. Heading back now, all jokes.
**Hilary:**   *(Looks at her empty glass)* Do you know, I've no idea why I did that.
**Joan:**   You've finished the sherry already?
**Hilary:**   When you suddenly said they were coming, I just threw it back.
**Joan:**   *(Amused)* But why?
**Hilary:**   *(Amused)* I must have been thinking of you choking on your Battenburg!
         *(Both enjoy this as Prentice begins to hurriedly drink his Guinness – as Vinny and Derek enter. They are in good mood, drinking off their drinks, Vinny smuggling in the bottle)*
**Vinny:**   *(Continuing business-like)* ... and that whole system carries a ten-year guarantee and can be installed in two days, three days maximum.
**Derek:**   It'll be my recommendation for the club, Vinny.
**Vinny:**   You won't be disappointed. *(Hears Hilary giggle. Now sees the mood)* Everything all right here,

                ladies?

**Hilary:**    Oh yes. Darling, we heard you in the loo.

**Derek:**    Pardon? Oh right – very impressive. *(Finally)* Well now, Hilary, if you've finished your drink we'll be on our way ...

**Hilary:**    *(Puts the water aside)* Just finished.

**Joan:**    I think Mr Prentice ...
                *(Derek and Vinny look at Prentice's three-quarter full glass)*

**Prentice:**    Won't be a minute. *(Tries to drink some)*

**Vinny:**    Oh. *(Watches Prentice try to drink some more)* Slow drinker, eh, Mr Prentice?

**Prentice:**    I was enjoying the chat.

**Vinny:**    Fine. *(To Joan)* And everything all right in ...? *(Indicates the kitchen)*

**Joan:**    What? Oh yes – it's on low heat.

**Vinny:**    Excellent. *(Waits)*

**Derek:**    *(Taps his stomach. To Vinny)* Ravenous.

**Vinny:**    *(To Derek)* Me too. Not long now.

**Derek:**    *(Quietly)* Stomach thinks my throat is cut.
                *(Vinny and Derek enjoy this – then silence as they wait patiently, while Prentice slowly tries to drink off his Guinness)*

**Hilary:**    *(Conversationally)* Mr Prentice was saying he knows someone who goes to your First Aid classes, darling.

**Derek:**    Oh really.

**Prentice:**    No, I only *think* I know.

**Hilary:**    Oh, I thought you said you knew her.

**Prentice:**    Oh I know her all right – but I only think that's where she goes.

**Derek:**    And who is that?

**Hilary:**    Her name's Patricia Mahony.

**Prentice:**    Mooney.

**Hilary:**    Mooney. Do you know her, darling?

**Derek:**    Never heard of her.

**Prentice:**    Everyone knows her as Patti.

**Hilary:**    He said she lives in the council houses.

**Derek:** Council houses? Don't think we have anyone from the council houses in our group.

**Vinny:** *(Lightly)* I wouldn't have thought you would.

**Derek:** Nor I.

**Prentice:** I'm not saying she goes – I only suspect she goes.

**Vinny:** *(Lightly)* Suspect? What makes you suspect?

**Derek:** *(Checks his watch)* I think I can clear this up and let Mr Prentice finish his drink, before we all go – there is no Patti Mooney in our First Aid group and, to the best of my knowledge, there never was.

**Vinny:** *(Finally)* There, that's that.

**Prentice:** So you don't know her. *(Drinks)*

**Derek:** *(Amused)* How many has he had?

**Joan:** *(Guiltily)* Oh just one. That one.

**Hilary:** *(Guiltily)* Yes, that's the only one.

**Derek:** Because I think I already said I never heard of her.

**Prentice:** I see.

**Derek:** What does that mean – 'I see'?

**Prentice:** No – just that I think she knows you.

**Derek:** Me?

**Prentice:** I think so.

**Derek:** What's her name again?

**Prentice:** Patti Mooney.

**Derek:** And this Patti Mooney said she knew me, did she?

**Prentice:** Well, no ...

**Derek:** Oh, she didn't say she knew me but she said she was in our First Aid group?

**Prentice:** No no, she never said that.

**Derek:** Then why are you coming to all these conclusions that we know each other?

**Hilary:** Would she know you from advertising, darling?

**Derek:** I've no idea.

**Prentice:** Ah no, it's just that I was talking to her once of a Thursday evening and she said she was waiting for someone ...

**Hilary:**    Mr Prentice says they're an old family in this area.

**Prentice:**  They used to own the top farm ...

**Hilary:**    Where Sycamore Crescent is now.

**Joan:**      Yes – *(To Prentice)* You told me that was once called Mooney's Field all right.

**Derek:**     Right – so she said she was waiting for whom?

**Prentice:**  She didn't say who.

**Vinny:**     *(Exasperated)* Not again!

**Derek:**     But it was one of our First Aid group?

**Prentice:**  I don't know that – but then you came along in your car ... and she got in.

**Derek:**     She got into my car?

**Prentice:**  Yes.

**Hilary:**    Where was this?

**Prentice:**  Down by the council houses.

**Derek:**     *(Amused)* You are saying that I was driving down by the council houses and you saw this Patti Mooney getting into my car?

**Prentice:**  It was months ago.

**Vinny:**     Where's your First Aid meetings held, Derek?

**Hilary:**    In Templeville, the opposite direction.

**Derek:**     *(To Prentice)* And what makes you think it was me you saw?

**Prentice:**  I just thought Patti must have been going to the First Aid with you ...

**Derek:**     But what makes you think it was me?

**Prentice:**  Well, I know your car.

**Derek:**     You know my car?

**Prentice:**  Yes – a big white one.

**Derek:**     A white one?

**Hilary:**    We don't have a white a car, Mr Prentice.

**Derek:**     My car is red – a blaze-red Volvo.

**Prentice:**  With an aerial-thing on the back.

**Vinny:**     Ah, an eir-cell phone ...

**Derek:**     Yes, I have an eir-cell phone ...

**Vinny:**     As do I, Derek – I'd be lost without it.

**Derek:**     But the car is blaze-red – not white.

**Hilary:** And mine is black.

**Vinny:** I've seen your's, Hilary – lovely little sports job.

**Derek:** So what have you got to say now, Mr Prentice?

**Prentice:** Well, if your car is red ...

**Derek:** It is red.

**Prentice:** Then it must have been someone else.

**Derek:** Well done. Now can we all get going?

**Joan:** Our car is white, Vinny.

**Vinny:** Sorry, Joan?

**Joan:** I'm just saying our car is white ...

**Prentice:** I know your car – it wasn't your's she got into.

**Vinny:** Well thank you very much – apart from the fact that I'm home every Thursday, I know nothing about First Aid and I never heard of Patti Murphy.

**Prentice:** Mooney.

**Vinny:** Mooney, Murphy, Mulligan or whatever her name is.

**Prentice:** Next time I see her, I'll ask her who he was.

**Derek:** Do that.

**Vinny:** *(Lightly)* And let us all know the answer – before our good ladies start suspecting us.

**Joan:** I never said I suspected ...

**Vinny:** That's a joke, Joan!

**Joan:** Oh.

**Vinny:** Right – so, finished now, Mr Prentice?

**Prentice:** *(Drinks up)* Yes.

**Derek:** Right, well I think we'll let you lead the way. Walking, are you?

**Prentice:** Oh yes, I like to walk. Good for the joints. *(Rubs his knees)* I'll go back now through Sycamore Avenue.

**Hilary:** Is there a road through the Avenue to your house?

**Prentice:** Oh not now – but I still like to keep to where the old lane-ways used to be – it's the ways myself and my mother always walked.

**Hilary:** Oh that's nice.

**Derek:**    (*Sharply*) Even though that'd now bring you in through the back gardens of Sycamore Avenue?

**Prentice:**  Ah, I don't think they mind.

**Derek:**    (*To Vinny*) See? Peeping.

**Prentice:**  So I'll be off.

**Joan:**     Thanks for coming.

**Hilary:**   And you never thought of getting a car, Mr Prentice?

**Prentice:**  Ah no ... they'd never give me a licence.

**Hilary:**   I got one.

**Joan:**     I'm thinking of taking lessons.

**Prentice:**  They still wouldn't give me one because, on top of everything else, I'm colour-blind: can't tell one colour from the next.

**Hilary:**   Well, here's a tip – remember the green traffic light is always on the bottom – nearest the green ground.

**Joan:**     (*Lightly*) That's very good Hilary – I must remember that for my test.

**Derek:**    (*Alerted*) Listen, something just crossed my mind – before we all gallop off, do you mind Vinny if I check-out a few security points with you ... ones that have just come to mind?

**Vinny:**    Security points, Derek?

**Derek:**    Just some clarification.

**Vinny:**    Of course.

**Hilary:**   Now, Derek?

**Derek:**    Won't take five minutes.

**Prentice:**  I'll be on my way so.

**Derek:**    I'd appreciate your opinion on this actually, Mr Prentice ...

**Prentice:**  Me?

**Derek:**    Yes – and Hilary, maybe Joan would like to show you the house while we men chat this over ...

**Vinny:**    That's a good idea, Joan – let Hilary see the new louvre doors in our master bedroom.

**Hilary:**   (*Annoyed*) Derek, I'm going to collapse with hunger!

**Derek:**      Five minutes!

**Prentice:**   I don't think I'll be much help.

**Derek:**      No, stay – we'll let the ladies indulge themselves
                and then we'll all be off.

**Hilary:**     *(Quietly to Derek)* Why now – with Mr Prentice?

**Derek:**      Five minutes – max ten, Hilary.

**Joan:**       Come on, Hilary – and I'll show you the picture
                of the horses galloping in the opposite direction.

**Hilary:**     *(To Derek)* Business, business, always business.

**Joan:**       *(Quietly)* And the Battenburg.

**Hilary:**     *(New note)* The Battenburg? Oh, right. *(Quieter)*
                Starving.

                *(Joan and Hilary go, closing the door)*

**Prentice:**   I think I'll be off ...

**Derek:**      Won't keep you a moment, Mr Prentice. Now,
                Vinny, does that door lock?

**Vinny:**      The door? Oh yes, both it and the kitchen door
                has a remote control locking system that ...

**Derek:**      Lock them so, will you?

**Vinny:**      Now?

**Derek:**      They lock from in here, don't they?

**Vinny:**      Oh yes and they're fire-proof and sound-proof
                and ...

**Derek:**      Let's just have that then.

**Vinny:**      Sure, Derek. Everything you see here has a ten-
                year, no-quibble guarantee ...

                *(Vinny presses the remote control. Both kitchen and
                entrance door lock)*

**Derek:**      Fine. Is that inter-room intercom thing turned off
                – like we can't be heard.

**Vinny:**      The system is totally tap-in proof: nobody can be
                overheard unless one party calls in and the other
                party connects it.

**Derek:**      Okay. Now I don't think either of us should beat
                around the bush here, Vinny.

**Vinny:**      About the security system?

**Derek:**      About what we've been hearing from your guest
                here – Mr Prentice.

**Vinny:**     Oh, Mr Prentice.

**Derek:**     As you know, I never liked the idea of him com-
               ing here ...

**Vinny:**     Well, it was Joan who ...

**Derek:**     But I have tried to be courteous – as you have,
               Vinny.

**Vinny:**     Oh, indeed.

**Derek:**     Despite him saying that your security system was
               irrelevant ...

**Vinny:**     Ah, but I can assure you that surveys show ...

**Derek:**     And despite hearing all about his carry-on with
               your wife while your back was turned ...

**Vinny:**     Joan?

**Derek:**     Or Mabel, as he likes to call her.

**Vinny:**     (Unsure) Oh well yes, that was a surprise ...

**Derek:**     But you choose not to say anything ...

**Vinny:**     Well no, because...

**Derek:**     Because you are a patient man, Vinny.

**Vinny:**     (Uneasy) Well, Joan often says ....

**Derek:**     However, I'm not like that.

**Vinny:**     Oh, I don't know.

**Derek:**     I play to win – and if anyone looks like trying to
               stop me ...

**Vinny:**     Oh, like at the squash ...?

**Derek:**     Exactly, like at the squash – you've seen what I've
               done to fellows who got it into their heads that
               they could take me on.

**Vinny:**     Oh I have.

**Derek:**     It always ends the same – me standing and they
               beaten into the ground. You see that's what hap-
               pens when I lose my patience with people who
               try to take me on ... and especially if they try to
               get smart. That's what really annoys me.

**Prentice:**  (Stands) I think I'll ...

**Derek:**     Now you sit down, Mr Prentice.

**Prentice:**  I'd prefer to go home, sir.

**Derek:**     And I'd prefer you to sit down. (Prentice sits)

**Vinny:**     Derek ...?

**Derek:**      *(Controlled)* Because there is no way you're walking out of this house after all the threats you just
made ...

**Prentice:**   I never ...

**Derek:**      ... in ways that you may think are smart, but I
don't. Let me take your glasses.
*(Derek reaches out to take Prentice's glasses)*

**Prentice:**   No, I can't see very well if you ...

**Derek:**      It's just for your own safety, Mr Prentice.

**Vinny:**      Derek, I thought we ...

**Derek:**      *(Takes them)* There. I'll put them here, out of the
way.

**Prentice:**   If they get broken ...

**Derek:**      Nothing need get broken – once you begin to use
a bit of common sense, Mr Prentice.

**Vinny:**      Derek, I thought we were going to discuss ...

**Derek:**      *(Continuing, to Prentice)* Like you know – don't
ask me how – that I'll be doing the advertising for
the extension of the estate. And the strange thing
was that as soon as that was decided, we all got
similar anonymous letters and Colm O'Reilly and
the developer had manure spread across their
cars. Now what do you say about that?

**Prentice:**   I'm saying nothing.

**Derek:**      Would you say they deserved it?

**Prentice:**   *(Then)* I would.

**Derek:**      And why's that now?

**Prentice:**   I'm not saying it was me – but I'm saying they deserved it for all the grabbin' they did – and now
I'd like to go.

**Derek:**      Grabbing? What grabbing?

**Prentice:**   Grabbing the land.

**Derek:**      What land is this now?

**Prentice:**   You know as well as I do – they came in and
grabbed the farmers' land for themselves and for
their cronies – but they'll grab no more and that's
all I'm saying.

**Derek:**      You're going to stop them?

**Prentice:** I am.

**Derek:** And what about me and the people who are employed by them?

**Prentice:** I'm saying no more.

**Derek:** *(Suddenly grabs Prentice)* By God, you're saying a lot more ...

**Prentice:** *(Angrily struggles)* Let me go ...

**Derek:** ... and about a lot more things than land.

**Prentice:** I'm saying nothing and you're doing nothing – not you or O'Reilly or any of you.

**Derek:** Going to stop us, are you?

**Prentice:** *(Furious)* Yes I am – this is not my mother you're dealing with ...! *(Stops)*

**Derek:** *(Lets go of him. Calmly)* Your mother? Oh this is about your mother, is it?

**Prentice:** Whether it is or not, I can tell you that extension road is not going through my land.

**Derek:** *(Calmly)* There's no way you can stop that road ...

**Prentice:** There is and my solicitor is about to tell the great Colm O'Reilly ...

**Derek:** There happens to be a Compulsory Purchase Order going through on that access property ...

**Prentice:** *(Suddenly furious)* It isn't 'access property', it's the last of my fields – and I can tell you I'm going to use every penny you paid my mother to stop you ever getting it – and then O'Reilly can go back to the developers and give back the back-handers they gave him – and the developers can look somewhere else to plunder and you will be left with only fields to advertise – and then you'll all have something else to worry about than squash clubs and Bar-B-Q's and speed ramps and Residents' Associations and whether you know Patti Mooney or not. This is going to put a stop to your gallop.
*(Pause)*

**Derek:** Feel better now?

**Prentice:** And I won't change my mind – nor will I hold my tongue if any of you try to go ahead.

**Derek:** Fine. Vinny, do you know what I think? I think we should let Mr Prentice see your dogs.

**Vinny:** My dogs?

**Derek:** Ah yes – it might take his mind off this for a while – give him time to re-think.

**Prentice:** I don't need time ...

**Derek:** Did you know Vinny had dogs, Mr Prentice?

**Prentice:** No.

**Derek:** What are they, Vinny? – A Doberman ...

**Vinny:** *(Unsure)* An Alsatian and a Rottweiler.

**Derek:** An Alsatian and a Rottweiler. Will we let Mr Prentice see them, Vinny?

**Vinny:** I don't think ...

**Derek:** Just the same as you did for me.

**Vinny:** Well, just to hear them then.
*(Vinny puts the control into his pocket)*

**Derek:** You like dogs, don't you, Mr Prentice?

**Prentice:** No.

**Derek:** No? Well. I think you'll like these. *(Winks at Vinny)* Come over to the window – then we'll chat again ... maybe with a bit more common sense.

**Prentice:** I'd prefer not to ...

**Derek:** It won't take a minute – *(Takes Prentice by the arm)* just see if you can see them.

**Prentice:** No, you see, I put on a bit of dinner at home ...

**Derek:** Vinny will make sure they do nothing ...

**Vinny:** They won't do a thing, Mr Prentice.

**Prentice:** I won't see them without my glasses.

**Derek:** Just try. You open the window for him, Vinny.

**Vinny:** Just to look out, Mr Prentice. *(As he opens the window)* They won't touch you at all, Mr Prentice – honestly.

**Derek:** You believe Vinny, don't you, Mr Prentice?

**Prentice:** *(Trying to struggle)* Maybe we should wait until Mabel comes back.

**Derek:** *(Towards Vinny)* Mabel? No, we'll let you look out

|            | now, before Mabel comes back ... |
|------------|----------------------------------|
| **Prentice:** | You're hurting my arm ... |
| **Derek:** | *(Releases him)* Oh very sorry ... |
| **Vinny:** | *(Nervously)* There's nothing to worry about ... |
| **Derek:** | *(At the window now)* Just lean out a bit – tell us what you see ... that's all. *(Prentice leans out)* Do you see Vinny's dogs? |
| **Prentice:** | It's very dark. |
| **Derek:** | Lean out further. |
| **Prentice:** | *(Looks back in)* I'm a bit afraid of dogs. |
| **Derek:** | Are you? *(Angrily grabs Prentice and pushes his head out)* Well, can you see them now? |
| **Prentice:** | *(Outside)* Let me in. |
| **Derek:** | *(Angrily)* And here's another question – did you see Patti Mooney getting into my car? *(Prentice suddenly begins to struggle. Derek holds him)* Hey? Did you? Did you? Let me hear you say 'No, Derek'. |
| **Prentice:** | Let me in. |
| **Derek:** | Wrong answer, Mr Prentice – I'm waiting for 'No, Derek'. |
| **Vinny:** | Derek, he'll hurt himself. |
| **Derek:** | Okay Vinny, bring on the dogs. |
| **Vinny:** | What? |
| **Derek:** | Whistle them in. Let the dogs get him. |
| **Prentice:** | No please ... |
| **Vinny:** | No Derek, he might hurt himself. |
| **Derek:** | Do it! |
| **Vinny:** | No, I can't ... |
| **Derek:** | *(Angrily)* Whistle the shaggin' things in – or you can forget all about the security in the squash club and everywhere else ... |
| **Prentice:** | Please ... |
| **Vinny:** | Maybe only in the distance ... |
| **Derek:** | Just get them on. |
|            | *(This as Vinny whistles, pressing his remote control. The dogs are heard in the distance)* |
| **Derek:** | Okay Prentice, can you hear them – they're com- |

ing to get you ...

**Prentice:** Please let me go ...

**Derek:** More, Vinny, more!

**Vinny:** No, that's enough!

**Derek:** *(To Vinny)* Come on! Get them to the window! Whistle!

*(Vinny whistles, bringing them very close, very loud, very savage. Prentice struggles. Derek holds him)*

**Derek:** Now, did you see Patti Mooney with me, did you?

**Prentice:** Please ...

**Derek:** Let me hear 'No Derek'.

**Prentice:** Let me in.

**Derek:** Did you see her – answer me! Are you giving us that field – answer me!

**Vinny:** He can't answer you!

**Derek:** He can if he wants! *(Pushes Prentice out further)* Okay let them get his face!

**Vinny:** Derek, for Christ's sake!

**Derek:** You won't destroy me, you bastard – I'll see you won't.

**Vinny:** You'll kill him for Christ's sake!

*(Derek suddenly pulls Prentice in)*

**Prentice:** Oh please ... don't ... I have a weak heart ...

**Derek:** Did you see Patti Mooney and me?

**Vinny:** He said he didn't.

**Derek:** He said he did to my bloody wife!

**Vinny:** No, he said it was a white car.

**Derek:** Then he said he was colour-blind.

**Vinny:** But you don't know her, do you?

**Derek:** Do I, Prentice, do I know her? Tell Vinny here – do I?

**Prentice:** *(Angrily)* You know bloody-well you know her!

**Derek:** Wrong answer – out you go again until you get it right!

*(Tries to push Prentice out again. Vinny suddenly grabs Derek. Prentice slumps to the ground as they struggle)*

**Vinny:**    Leave him ...

**Derek:**    Get your hands off me ...

**Vinny:**    He said he has a weak heart ...

**Derek:**    Get your hands off me ...

*(Derek pulls free. Vinny falls and now tries to get out his remote control. Prentice has been crawling towards the door)*

**Prentice:**   Mabel! Mabel! Help me!

*(Derek grabs him to drag him back to the window)*

**Derek:**    I'll make sure you say nothing ...

**Prentice:**   And I'm closing the road, once and for all.

**Derek:**    And I'm closing your mouth, once and for all.

*(Vinny presses the buttons. The dogs stop)*

[*To Vinny*] What are you at – turn them on.

**Vinny:**    No – this has gone far enough.

*(Derek throws Vinny aside, grabs the small control and angrily presses buttons. Getting no reaction, he will throw the small one against the wall and grab the main control)*

**Derek:**    *(To Vinny)* And you're finished too – you spineless little moron.

**Prentice:**   *(Points to Derek)* I'll tell everybody about your Thursdays and poor Hilary.

**Derek:**    *(Struggling with the control)* How does these shaggin' things work?

**Prentice:**   *(Points to Vinny)* And you and your sperm-count and poor Mabel!

**Vinny:**    *(Stops)* What did you say?!

*(At this moment, Derek has flung the main control aside and angrily kicks the console. Immediately, the system goes awry: we hear the dogs very loud – also the scream of jet planes through the room and a quick flashing of the lights. In this flashing, we see Derek hit out at Prentice. Prentice takes the blows and falls. Vinny has now grabbed the control, pressed buttons. Cut all sounds of dogs, lights and jets)*

**Derek:**    *(Angrily)* Turn that on!

**Vinny:**    *(Angrily grabs Prentice)* What did you just say?

How did you know about that?

**Derek:** Know about what?

**Vinny:** *(Angrily)* I'm talking to you, Prentice – who told you about that? *(Prentice is immobile)* Prentice? *(Shakes him)* Mr Prentice? *(No move)* Mr Prentice? *(To Derek)* He's not ...?

**Derek:** *(Kneels)* Prentice?

**Vinny:** Oh my God.

**Derek:** Mr Prentice. Come on. Wake up.

**Vinny:** He doesn't seem to be ...

**Derek:** *(Stands back)* Jesus. You must have hurt him when you...

**Vinny:** I hardly touched him. Is he all right? He said he had a weak heart ...

**Derek:** *(Moves away from him)* Mr Prentice, are you all right?

**Vinny:** Examine him!

**Derek:** You examine him!

**Vinny:** Me? You're in the First Aid – you're the one with the stethoscope.

**Derek:** Shut-up about that! Mr Prentice?

**Vinny:** Every Thursday you're practising for this kind of thing...

**Derek:** I said shut-up. Is he breathing at all?

**Vinny:** You mean you don't ...?

**Derek:** *(Quietly)* Prentice, please open your eyes.

**Vinny:** But you must know something. You were at Hilary's birth, in the delivery room ...

**Derek:** *(Looking at Prentice)* Jesus, he's not breathing.

**Vinny:** Remember the vegetable – how your son would have been a vegetable if you didn't tell the gynaecologist. ..

**Derek:** Will you shut-up – I wasn't there.

**Vinny:** You were there ...

**Derek:** I wasn't! I was there at the beginning but then I fainted ...

**Vinny:** Fainted?

**Derek:** They had to carry me out ... it was another doctor that Hilary heard shouting.

**Vinny:** What?!

**Derek:** I have to say these things because she wants me to be a doctor ...

**Vinny:** (*Angrily grabs Derek*) What did you say?

**Derek:** (*Angrily pulls free*) All right – for Christ's sake, the guy she was going to marry was a doctor, so ...

**Vinny:** So you know nothing?

**Derek:** Prentice, please don't do this ...

**Vinny:** And you wanted to be at Joan's delivery – keeping an eye on her things?

**Derek:** I didn't! I don't want to be at anyone's delivery – I can't stand that sort of thing.

**Vinny:** Well, that's great – that's terrific – and now look at what you've done!

**Derek:** (*Breaks down in sudden sobs of panic*) Oh God, oh Christ, I'm ruined, destroyed ... I'll be finished in the club, on the committee, the police will want to know ... Hilary ... her family ... Oh God, oh Christ, I'm ruined ...

**Vinny:** (*Suddenly taking over*) Listen – stop! First of all, don't panic. (*Then*) We'll say he fainted ...

**Derek:** Fainted? There's blood on his head ...

**Vinny:** We'll say he hit his head ... looking at the dogs ... the way you did ... and then he fainted.

**Derek:** What? Yes. Right. We could say that ... and that sounds right because I had said I wanted to check the security...so that's why we had the dogs on ...

**Vinny:** Exactly. Then when Joan and Hilary get back, we can ask them to help us revive him ...?

**Derek:** (*Panic*) Revive him? How can they revive him if ...?

**Vinny:** Stay calm!

**Derek:** Right, right – I'm calm ...

**Vinny:** Then when he doesn't come round for them, then we'll call a doctor ...

**Derek:** Right. Freddie Dawson. He's in the club, on the committee, chairman of the Residents' Association ...

**Vinny:** Okay, but all the time we have to keep remembering that it was an accident ...

**Derek:** Oh right – no one meant for this to happen ...

**Vinny:** He just happened to hit his head the way you did ...

**Derek:** Looking at the security. Great. Fine. Well done. *(Then)* And Vinny, when we get through this, I'll look after you in the club, on the committee, that sort of thing...

**Vinny:** Never mind that now ...

**Derek:** No, that's a promise – when we get the road through the estate, and we will ... I 'll see that you get all the security contracts ...

**Vinny:** Listen let's get this done first ...

**Derek:** You're right ... as I said before: it's not the mistakes we make, but how we correct them ... and you really are Mr Fix-It, Vinny – you really are one great Mr Fix-It.

**Vinny:** Right. Now, better unlock that door ...
*(Vinny presses the remote control. The locks click back)*

**Derek:** Right. And Freddie Dawson will see that it's an accident ... we know Freddie well ...

**Vinny:** And maybe I better call the ladies back now ... break the news to them gently.

**Derek:** The ladies – right. *(Nervously)* And no panic. Total accident.

**Vinny:** Exactly. *(Into the intercom)* Calling Joan in master bedroom. *(No reply. Presses another button)* Calling Joan in morning room. *(No reply. Presses another button)* Calling Joan in reading room..

**Joan:** *(v/o)* What, Vinny. *(Coughs)* Excuse me. Over.

**Vinny:** Joan, are you eating something there?

**Joan:** *(v/o. She clearly is)* No. We heard the dogs.

**Vinny:** Oh yes – Derek wanted to hear them ...

**Derek:** *(Prompts)* And him!

**Vinny:** ... and Mr Prentice wanted to hear them too.

**Joan:**     *(v/o)* Oh great. Was he surprised?

**Vinny:**    Well, as a matter of fact, he fainted.

**Joan:**     *(v/o)* Fainted?

**Vinny:**    Yes, but he's fine, still weak but Derek's looking at him, says he's grand ... and I think he'll be going home soon.

**Joan:**     Are you sure, Vinny?

**Vinny:**    Absolutely – he's sitting here chatting to us ... hold on, he's saying something ... *(Loudly)* Pardon, Mr Prentice? *(Waits. Then, to Joan)* Yes, he just said you're not to worry, that he's grand.

**Joan:**     *(v/o)* Oh right – we'll just look at the conservatory and we'll be down before he goes.

**Vinny:**    Excellent.

**Joan:**     *(v/o)* And Vinny, Hilary loves the house.

**Hilary:**   *(v/o. Background. Also eating and giggling)* Oh yes, Vinny – it's delicious. I mean it's lovely.

**Vinny:**    Great. Over and out so. *(Switches off)*

**Derek:**    That was good, Vinny – very calm.

**Vinny:**    Right. Now maybe you should be examining him.

**Derek:**    *(Panic)* Not if he's ....

**Vinny:**    They'll come in thinking he's fainted!

**Derek:**    Oh right. Right. I hate doing this. *(Takes out his stethoscope. Then puts it to Prentice's chest)* Oh God, not a sound. He really is, you know – I know that much. *(Takes it away)*

              *(Vinny will now busily take Mr Prentice's glasses from the table and carefully place them on Prentice's face. Then he will tidy the room and close the window)*

**Vinny:**    When did you get that thing anyway?

**Derek:**    Years ago – to convince Hilary about the Thursdays.

**Vinny:**    Desperate carry-on.

**Derek:**    Don't start that.

**Vinny:**    I'm not, I'm not. *(Then)* And what about all the trophies you won.

**Derek:**    Bought them. Had them all engraved myself. *(Then)* But we were always so bloody careful.

| | |
|---|---|
| **Vinny:** | Picking her up in the street? |
| **Derek:** | It was in the council houses. And we always cleared off – I always insisted we go to Gaston's Hotel. |
| **Vinny:** | Gaston's Hotel? – that must be forty miles away. |
| **Derek:** | Exactly – and we always called ourselves Mr and Mrs Matthews. Well, that was Patti's little joke – she said Matthews sounded like 'mattress' and we always had Commodore mattresses in Gastons. |
| **Vinny:** | *(Coldly)* Great sense of humour. |
| **Derek:** | *(Bitterly)* When she wasn't cracking stupid jokes she was trying to talk me into leaving Hilary. |
| **Vinny:** | Leaving Hilary? |
| **Derek:** | Yeah – some chance I'd have of surviving, without Hilary's money. Stupid little bitch. |
| **Vinny:** | *(Listens at the door)* Quick – start examining him. |
| **Derek:** | Right. I really hate this. *(Puts the stethoscope to Prentice's chest again)* I had to stop listening to Patti's heart because the gurgling sound of it used make me sick. |
| **Vinny:** | And stop talking about her! |
| **Derek:** | *(Listens)* Jesus – silence. |
| | *(The door opens. Joan and Hilary come in – Hilary carries a piece of wallpaper. Their mood is lively)* |
| **Joan:** | Say you need it for a room that gets plenty of sunlight ... |
| **Hilary:** | It's really lovely ... |
| **Joan:** | *(Sees Prentice)* Oh my God, Mr Prentice! |
| **Vinny:** | It's all right, Joan – he only fainted. |
| **Joan:** | But I thought you said he came round again. |
| **Vinny:** | He did, for a while ... |
| **Derek:** | *(Listening)* Coming around again now ... |
| **Vinny:** | In fact, he was talking a minute ago ... |
| **Hilary:** | He looks like death. |
| **Derek:** | No no, he's fine – just hit his head, the very way I did ... |
| **Hilary:** | It looks really nasty ... |

**Derek:**    Just a slight concussion – but the heart is strong ...
              *(Stands)*
**Vinny:**    And that's what counts ...
**Joan:**     *(Kneeling)* Mr Prentice ...?
**Vinny:**    Derek suggests we leave him as he is and maybe
              ring a doctor ...
**Joan:**     A doctor? I thought you said ...
**Derek:**    Just a second opinion. *(To Hilary)* I was thinking
              of maybe Freddie Dawson.
**Hilary:**   Oh yes, I really think we should.
**Derek:**    But no great urgency ... in my estimation.
**Joan:**     I wish he'd come round ...
**Vinny:**    *(Takes Joan away)* Derek knows about these things,
              Joan.
**Hilary:**   *(To Joan)* He really does. He practises this all the
              time.
**Derek:**    *(Confidently)* Now, might have a drink – then I'll
              give Freddie a ring.
**Vinny:**    Yes – might have one as well ...
**Joan:**     God, I'd be more worried ...
**Hilary:**   *(To Joan)* Well so would I – but Derek is really
              used to this ... you should see the trophies he has.
**Derek:**    *(At the drinks)* And you like the house, do you,
              Hilary?
**Hilary:**   *(Looking at Prentice)* Pardon?
**Derek:**    The house – you like it?
**Hilary:**   Oh yes, it's lovely – you are sure, Derek?
**Derek:**    Absolutely. Mild concussion.
**Vinny:**    *(Trying)* Took a sample of the wallpaper I see.
**Hilary:**   *(Concerned)* Oh yes – your morning room.
**Joan:**     *(Cannot contain her concern)* I'll look-up the doctor
              in the phone-book – what's his name again?
**Vinny:**    Freddie Doyle.
**Derek:**    Dawson.
**Vinny:**    Dawson.
**Derek:**    But no real need – no real urgency.
              *(Joan has gone to the phone book)*
**Hilary:**   Do you know, darling, I think you are right.

**Derek:** About what, darling?

**Hilary:** Mr Prentice. He's opening his eyes.

**Derek:** *(Stops)* Who is?

**Hilary:** Mr Prentice – hello Mr Prentice.

**Joan:** *(Goes to him)* So he is. Hello Mr Prentice. *(Prentice moves)*

**Vinny:** *(Looks)* Jesus.

**Hilary:** *(To Derek)* Oh darling – you were right – your diagnosis was absolutely right. I should have trusted you.

*(Derek looks stunned)*

**Joan:** *(To Prentice)* Let me fix your glasses properly.

**Vinny:** *(To Derek)* He's alive!

*(Prentice now tries to sit up. He has blood on his head)*

**Joan:** Mr Prentice, how do you feel?

**Prentice:** Oh my God ... My head ... My head is pounding like a drum ...

**Joan:** You hit it on the window.

**Hilary:** Do you want to examine him, darling?

**Derek:** Examine him? No no, he's all right.

**Prentice:** *(Very groggy)* Where am I at all?

**Joan:** Forty-four Sycamore, Mr Prentice. We were very worried about you.

**Hilary:** You were listening to the dogs and you banged your head.

**Prentice:** What dogs are you talking about?

**Joan:** He doesn't remember. Do you know who I am?

**Prentice:** *(To Vinny)* What did she say?

**Vinny:** She's ... she's asking if you know who she is.

**Prentice:** Who's she?

**Vinny:** She? That's Joan.

**Joan:** Mabel.

**Prentice:** *(Trying to focus)* Ah Mabel, it's you, is it?

**Hilary:** He remembers. *(To Prentice)* Yes. Do you remember Vinny? This is Vinny.

**Prentice:** *(Trying to focus)* Are you Mabel's husband?

**Joan:** Yes!

**Hilary:** Ah, that's better. And now do you remember

Derek? Der-ek.

**Derek:** (*Uneasily*) Hello, Mr Prentice.

**Prentice:** (*Pleasantly*) Oh hello, sir.

**Hilary:** His name is Derek. And I'm Hilary. Derek attended you, Mr Prentice – made you better.

**Prentice:** My head is still pounding ...

**Joan:** Will he be all right, Derek?

**Derek:** (*To Prentice*) You say you don't remember the dogs, Mr Prentice – listening to the dogs?

**Prentice:** I don't know any dogs. (*Then*) Did I finish my Guinness?

**Joan:** You did – look here's the empty glass.

**Prentice:** Ah, yes. What happened then ... my head is pounding like a drum.

**Vinny:** Maybe he's had a complete blank since then.

**Joan:** Since when?

**Vinny:** Since he had that drink.

**Hilary:** Did he, Derek?

**Derek:** What? (*Authoritatively*) Yes, yes I think that is very likely. Probably an amnesia since then.

**Prentice:** (*Struggles*) Get to my feet ...

**Joan:** Take it easy, Mr Prentice ...

**Hilary:** Should he, Derek?

**Derek:** If he can, yes. (*Helps him to a chair*) There you are now. Tell me, how do you feel?

**Prentice:** Bit dizzy – and a bit weak on the oul pins ...

**Derek:** But you can't remember since your drink ...

**Prentice:** Just this pounding in my head.

**Derek:** Fine. (*To all, professionally and confidentially*) He's grand – I think his memory could be gone but even if he remembers anything, it could be very confused, maybe imagining things that never really happened at all.

**Vinny:** Oh that wouldn't surprise me at all.

**Derek:** If that happens – if he begins to talk about things he *thinks* happened to himself or to others, I feel that's best ignored – otherwise, he's grand.

**Hilary:** Oh good. Mr Prentice, would you like Derek to

|  | perhaps drive you home? |
| Joan: | Or you could lie down here for a few hours ... |
| Prentice: | Thanks very much – but maybe I'll walk – get the circulation going. |
| Derek: | Fresh air will do him good. |
| Vinny: | Exactly. |
| Hilary: | You won't fall, will you? |
| Prentice: | I think I'll be grand now – and thanks for inviting me over, Mabel. |
| Joan: | Sure you only had a drink. *(Shakes hands. Jokes)* Or two ... |
| Prentice: | Next time maybe I'll stay longer. |
| Joan: | Oh do. |
| Hilary: | We really enjoyed meeting you, Mr Prentice. *(Shakes hands)* |
| Derek: | Yes indeed – and we're all heading off home now anyway *(lightly to Vinny)* said he, ravenously. |
| Vinny: | Oh right. *(Nods to the kitchen)* Joan? Everything okay? |
| Joan: | *(Remembers)* Oh God! *(Joan wants to go to the kitchen – but waits as Prentice speaks)* |
| Prentice: | Or better still, maybe I'll take ye all out for a drink or something sometime – to make up for this. |
| Vinny: | Not at all ... *(Laughs to Derek)* We won't push our luck. |
| Derek: | *(Laughs)* No, leave well enough alone. |
| Prentice: | But I'd like to. Maybe we'd all go out for an evening – to maybe, Gaston's Hotel, all on me? |
| Hilary: | *(Lightly)* But that's nearly forty miles away! |
| Joan: | *(Urgently)* Mr Prentice, I have to dash ... |
| Prentice: | I'll see you on our walks. |
| Joan: | Of course. *(To Hilary)* Forgot all about the oven! *(Joan runs to the kitchen)* |
| Hilary: | Let me help, Joan ... |
| Joan: | No, I'm all right ... |
| Hilary: | No, I do love to pitch in ... |

*(Hilary follows Joan into the kitchen)*

**Prentice:**  I'll be off so ...

**Derek:**  Hold on. What's this about Gaston's Hotel? What was that about?

**Prentice:**  Just we could maybe go there some evening – all of us, on me.

**Derek:**  But why Gaston's?

**Prentice:**  Why not? We could pick a convenient evening and go up. Maybe a Thursday, if you're free.

**Vinny:**  Did he ...?

**Derek:**  How much do you remember?

**Prentice:**  I don't remember anything ...

**Derek:**  *(Controlled)* That's right, you don't – and if you do, it's no more than you knew before – and that's just your word against mine ... so don't you try anything smart ... or you could be taught another lesson very quickly.

**Prentice:**  That's the way it used to be.

**Derek:**  That's the way it is.

**Prentice:**  No no, it's changed now; now we go to Gaston's Hotel and ask the staff there if any of them recognises Mr and Mrs Matthews.

**Vinny:**  Christ!

**Derek:**  How did you ... (know about that?)

**Prentice:**  And Patti Mooney might like to know why you'll never leave your wife ...

**Derek:**  What?

**Prentice:**  And your wife might like to know why you have that stethoscope or where you got all your trophies ...

**Vinny:**  He heard it all.

**Derek:**  *(To Vinny)* Yes he did and it's all your bloody fault.

**Vinny:**  Mine? It wasn't me that went out with Patti.

**Derek:**  It was you asked me all those bloody questions in front of him.

**Vinny:**  Only because you said he was dead.

**Derek:**  So did you!

**Vinny:** You listened to his heart.

**Prentice:** He was listening to the wrong side! *(Indicates his right-side chest)*

**Derek:** I was not!

**Prentice:** You were so.

**Derek:** I was not!

**Vinny:** And you're supposed to be the doctor.

**Derek:** I'm not a bloody doctor.

**Vinny:** Oh you can say that again!.

**Derek:** *(Furiously to Vinny)* But you're finished ... in the club, in the estate, in the town, everywhere. I'll see to it that nobody even buys a door-bell from you!

*(Furious silence. Then)*

**Prentice:** Of course, I needn't say anything to anyone about anything.

**Derek:** *(Turns. Suddenly calm)* What? Yes ... Right ... and I'd really appreciate that, Mr Prentice ...

**Prentice:** Provided we come to some arrangement ...

**Derek:** *(Hope)* Arrangement? Of course, yes ... and I'd appreciate it if Hilary never knew ...

**Prentice:** Like the developers paying me the full money they should have gave to my mother for grabbing her land ...

**Derek:** *(Doubtful)* Well now ...

**Prentice:** And a nice, big plaque to her memory put on the sycamore tree ...

**Derek:** *(Pleading)* Look, Mr Prentice ...

**Prentice:** If I got that, maybe we could discuss the access road and you doing the advertising and then maybe we could forget all about Gaston's Hotel ...

**Derek:** Let's first forget about Gaston's Hotel!

**Prentice:** *(Moves)* Or maybe I'll go ... and write a few anonymous letters to people's wives ...

**Derek:** No no, wait – let's work something out ... better still, why don't you stay here for a chat over a relaxed dinner ...

**Vinny:** What?

**Prentice:** I already have a bit of dinner on ...

**Derek:** You could leave that – Vinny, you could fit another in here tonight ...

**Vinny:** How the hell can I ...?

**Prentice:** We can't ask Mabel to start making dinners ...

**Vinny:** Her name's Joan!

**Derek:** No, it can be Mabel! *(To Prentice)* The truth is, there was an option on a bite to eat here, so let's take that up – I always believe that business is best after a relaxing dinner *(Looks to the kitchen)* – and I know we can keep all this between ourselves ...

**Prentice:** Only provided the business talks go well ...

**Derek:** And they will, never fear.

**Prentice:** *(To Vinny)* And only provided you arrange to go for your check-up.

**Vinny:** What?

**Prentice:** It's not 'what' it's 'pardon'.

**Derek:** What check-up is this?

**Prentice:** Mabel's husband knows.

**Vinny:** *(To Prentice, annoyed)* Yes he does and he'd like to know how you know anything about ...?

**Prentice:** And provided you never tell her I suggested it *(To Derek)* ... or the whole arrangement is off ...

**Derek:** No, no, it's not off. *(Looks anxiously to the kitchen)*

**Prentice:** ... in which case, we'll all be going to Gaston's to see who recognises who ...

**Derek:** Now that's what we don't want!

**Prentice:** *(To Derek)* Then he does what I'm asking.

**Vinny:** I will not – I want to know how you know ...

**Derek:** No you don't! *(To Prentice)* Vinny will do exactly what you say ...

**Vinny:** No, I won't and I want to know ....

**Derek:** Vinny, we haven't much time – you do whatever the hell it is and, in return, I can here-and-now guarantee that your security system ...
*(Both Hilary and Joan come from the kitchen. They carry plates of pizzas, cutlery, etc. Both stop, embar-*

*rassed, on seeing Prentice)*

**Hilary:** Oh dear – we thought you were gone, Mr Prentice ...

**Derek:** No no, actually Joan, we were hoping he'd maybe stay for dinner.

**Joan:** Dinner ...?!

**Derek:** I said we had an option on a bite to eat ...

**Joan:** *(To Vinny)* But we only got four pizzas because you said ...

**Derek:** That's okay, he can have mine.

**Hilary:** But darling, you're starving ...

**Derek:** No – I'm not hungry at all ...

**Prentice:** Or maybe I'll go home after all ...

**Derek:** No no, please stay.

**Hilary:** *(To Prentice)* Is this because Derek attended to you so well, Mr Prentice?

**Derek:** Yes, that's it – we feel we'd like to chat on.

**Hilary:** Lovely – that's the patient/doctor relationship.

**Derek:** Exactly.

**Hilary:** Well, I'm starving and this looks delicious.

**Joan:** I hope you all like it ...

**Derek:** I am certain we will ... *they* will.

**Joan:** *(To Prentice)* We're having it in the television room ...

**Hilary:** I know where that is so I'll lead on ...

**Derek:** *(Holds the door open)* Allow me, darling.

**Hilary:** *(Proudly)* Thank you, doctor. *(Goes)*

**Derek:** *(Holds the door for Prentice)* After you, Mr Prentice.

**Prentice:** Thank you ... doctor.

*(Prentice goes. Derek follows. Joan is about to follow)*

**Vinny:** *(Angrily)* Joan! Come here!

**Joan:** But we're all going in to ...

**Vinny:** *(Closes the door)* That can wait until you bloody-well explain something to me!

**Joan:** It wasn't me that told Mr Prentice to stay.

**Vinny:** *(Angrily)* To hell with that – I want to know how he knows something that only you could have told him.

**Joan:**     What?
            *(The door opens. Derek looks in)*
**Derek:**    Vinny?
**Vinny:**    *(Angrily)* What?!
**Derek:**    Just nipped back to say that's now a one-hundred per cent guarantee: your security system goes into the club. Wanted to make that clear.
**Joan:**     Oh Vinny, that's great.
**Derek:**    Allow me, Joan. *(Takes Joan's tray)*
**Joan:**     Oh thanks, Derek.
**Derek:**    Pleasure, Joan. And, Vinny, once we get the new extension going, your system goes in there too. Also one-hundred per cent guaranteed.
**Joan:**     Vinny, I'm delighted.
**Derek:**    Provided, you know ... *before* we sit down.
**Vinny:**    *(Reluctantly and angrily)* Yeah. Right. Okay.
**Derek:**    Excellent. *(Turns to go. Stops. Pointed)* Remember, Vinny, it's not the mistakes we make, but how we correct them. *(Derek goes)*
**Vinny:**    *(Angrily)* Jesus!
**Joan:**     *(Delighted)* But Vinny, this is great ...
**Vinny:**    Will you let me think!
**Joan:**     Oh Vinny, it's great and I'm really delighted for you. You see, I was terrible worried in case ...
**Vinny:**    Joan ...
**Joan:**     ... he wouldn't like the security system and then that'd be all my fault because ...
**Vinny:**    Joan ...
**Joan:**     ... I was letting you down all the time by not being able to cook and not being able to contribute and ...
**Vinny:**    Joan, will you listen! *(Then reluctantly)* I just want to say one thing.
**Joan:**     Oh – what, Vinny?
**Vinny:**    I'm going to ring the hospital tomorrow.
**Joan:**     Why, do you not feel well?
**Vinny:**    *(An effort)* To go for that ... check-up.
**Joan:**     Oh Vinny – seriously?

**Vinny:** Yeah. Okay?

**Joan:** Oh Vinny – thanks. *(Kisses him)* And Vinny, I want to tell you something: I'm really glad we're living in Sycamore – I really am.

**Vinny:** *(Annoyed but resigned)* Are you now!

**Joan:** *(Warmly)* Oh yes. And everything is going to be great – wait'll you see.

**Vinny:** *(Turns to go)* Come on before the food gets cold.

**Joan:** I'll just get a plate and cutlery for Mr Prentice.

*(As soon as Vinny has gone, Joan goes excitedly to the phone and dials out)*

**Joan:** Ma? Oh ma, it's going great. Mr Prentice is staying for dinner ... and Derek says he's going to buy Vinny's security system ... and Vinny says he's going to go for that check-up tomorrow and Hilary is really lovely – and best of all, her and me are planning a secret surprise for Vinny and Derek and Mr Prentice. Listen! We're going to take them out for dinner, by taxis, and we're telling them nothing until we get there – and we want you to come too. It's only to a hotel that Mr Prentice likes called Gastons.

*(Now we hear the music of Phil Harris singing 'Forty-four Sycamore' as Joan excitedly continues: 'Come on ma, it'll be great ... you'll really enjoy it ...' Through this, the music comes up as we fade to darkness ... hearing the music to the end.)*

## THE END

# THE LAST APACHE REUNION

*This play was first produced at the Abbey Theatre Dublin on 25 May 1993 with the following cast:*

| | |
|---|---|
| HARRY | Don Wycherley |
| DEIRDRE | Jane Brennan |
| JIMMY | Mark O'Regan |
| MAURICE | Arthur Riordan |
| NICK | Frank McCusker |
| JACKIE | Lise-Ann McLaughlin |
| PAUDGE | David Herlihy |
| KEVIN | Aidan McArdle |
| | |
| DIRECTOR | Ben Barnes |
| DESIGNER | Frank Hallinan Flood |
| LIGHTING | Rupert Murray |

*FOR THERESE*

# ACT ONE
# SCENE ONE

*A classroom – old, unused and neglected. Desks and chairs piled carelessly. A blackboard on the stage-left wall. Two windows in the back wall. Their design (built-in wooden shutters) tells us that the building is maybe a hundred years old. The window shutters are folded open.*

*The room used to be very big – but now a floor-to-ceiling wooden partition crudely cuts it in half. This partition is our stage-right wall. It has a door in it. The entrance door is in the opposite stage-left wall.*

*The classroom is on the second floor. It is a stormy night. Rain beats against the window. Occasionally rumbles of thunder and some lightning. It is 11:30 p.m. summer.*

*At the start, all is dark. Then a flash of lightning lights up the room and thunder rumbles away as the entrance door is opened. Light from the corridor shows us Harry. He steps in and finds the light switch. The over-hanging lights come on. We see that Harry is 32, overweight, well-dressed in a suit. He is an extrovert man. He carries some six-packs.*

**Harry:**    *(To himself)* Brilliant! *(Shouts back)* Jimmy? – up here – it's this one up here. And the electricity's on here too.
*(He wanders in, looking around in awe)*
That partition is new ... there was a map of the world on that wall ... the blackboard still there ... my desk was there ... *(Private joke: hand up like a little boy)* An bhfuil cead agam dul amac, mar se do thuile. *(Looks around)* And in a week, it'll all be a heap of rubble. *(Moved)* Ghosts everywhere. If these walls could talk, what would they say?
*(Deirdre's head has appeared around the door. She is 30, homely, well-dressed for a night out. She carries an umbrella)*

**Deirdre:**  Hello.

**Harry:**  *(Shock)* Oh Jaysus! *(Then)* Oh hello, come in, come in – you're Jimmy's wife, aren't you?

**Deirdre:**  Yes: Deirdre – Jimmy must be looking around downstairs. And you're Harry.

**Harry:**  That's it: Harry Lawless. *(Shakes hands)* Didn't really get a chance to say hello in the pub.

**Deirdre:**  No – like sardines down there.

**Harry:**  Always the same – but I could see you over in the corner ...

**Deirdre:**  Oh I didn't mind – Jimmy was pointing you all out to me.

**Harry:**  The old gang, eh? – well you just wait and see us in action here tonight: we'll finish up wrecking this old school before the demolition crowd even get near it. *(Kicks over a chair)*

**Deirdre:**  *(Not impressed)* Lovely – but I understood we were all going back to Maurice's house.

**Harry:**  We were, until I had my brainwave: forget Maurice's house – have the reunion here.

**Deirdre:**  Oh that was your brainwave, was it?

**Harry:**  And when you think about it, Deirdre, it's obvious. No disrespect to Maurice, but bringing booze back to his house is like bringing a Karioke machine into a Trappist monastery: doomed before it starts.

**Deirdre:**  Really?

**Harry:**  Absolutely. But now, seriously, straight out, what do you think of this place for the reunion?

**Deirdre:**  *(Mannerly)* Well it's ...

**Harry:**  I know – historic. That's exactly what I said down in the pub. That old school, I said, lying empty up there, due to be demolished in a few week's time – if we can break a lock or two and if the electricity is still on, then it's ideal for the first reunion of the Apaches.

**Deirdre:**  Well yes but it's ...

**Harry:**  You knew the five of us were called the Apaches

|            | at school, didn't you?                                    |
|------------|-----------------------------------------------------------|

**Deirdre:** Well not until ...

**Harry:** (*Looking around*) Nick was called Running Bear, Paudge was Sitting Bull, I was called Crazy Horse – and you'll soon see why! Hey, did you hear me singing our song down in the pub?

**Deirdre:** Well it was so crowded I ...

**Harry:** (*Sings and stomps*) 'On the banks of the River, stood Running Bear, young Indian brave ...'

**Deirdre:** Oh yes ...

**Harry:** That was our song in this very room – so are you getting the picture, Deirdre: fifteen years ago five guys walk out of here as impressionable school-boys, tonight they return as five mature, success-ful businessmen. What business is Jimmy in, by the way?

**Deirdre:** Oh he's actually a pest control specialist.

**Harry:** Terrific. Now you guess what line I'm in – bearing in mind now all my brainwaves and my sense of organisation?

**Deirdre:** Are you ... ?

**Harry:** Right – travel. Partnership in a world-wide travel firm – specialise in family holidays, to Spain and Portugal mostly. You got a family, Deirdre?

**Deirdre:** Well we've three sons ...

**Harry:** Great discount for kids – I'll leave you my card (*Flicks it from his pocket*) – phone the office or phone me anytime, I'm on the mobile – and tell Jimmy. Where did he get to – wasn't your car just behind me coming in?

**Deirdre:** Yes – I thought he ...

**Harry:** Don't worry, I'll find him – you settle in. You won't be afraid in here on your own, will you?

**Deirdre:** No, no ...

**Harry:** Right. (*Lightly*) They used to say it was a funny old building but, Deirdre, if any of the ghosts of the last hundred years appear, you just scream. (*Goes*) Jimmy? Apaches? Up here.

*(Deirdre is left to look in disgust at the room. As she does, there is a crack of thunder and, in the lightning, a face ghostily appears outside the window. A man. This is Jimmy. He taps on the window. Deirdre turns and sees him and cries out with fright)*

**Jimmy:** *(Outside)* Open the window!

**Deirdre:** Jimmy! What are you doing out there?

**Jimmy:** Open the shaggin' window!

*(Deirdre pulls up the window. Jimmy climbs in. He is 32, small and greying. His suit is now wet and dishevelled)*

**Deirdre:** Jimmy, how did you get out there?

**Jimmy:** I didn't get out – I climbed up the drainpipe.

**Deirdre:** The drainpipe? From the ground?

**Jimmy:** No, I flew halfway up first – of course from the bloody ground. *(Anxiously)* Is Harry not here – I wanted Harry to see me climbing in.

**Deirdre:** For what?

**Jimmy:** Because, Deirdre, this is what I always did – I was up and down that drainpipe more than I was in and out the door – this is why the Apaches always called me Little Squirrel.

**Deirdre:** God, you're beginning to sound like Harry.

**Jimmy:** Were you talking to him?

**Deirdre:** More like listening to him talking to himself – before he galloped off to find you.

**Jimmy:** Great guy – Harry. This was our old classroom, Deirdre ... just look at it.

**Deirdre:** I am – and I don't want to look at it much longer.

**Jimmy:** *(Looks around)* It is a monument to all that is past. Make sure you tell the lads about Little Squirrel climbing up the drainpipe: they'll be proud of me doing that.

**Deirdre:** I'd be happy to climb down it this minute and go home.

**Jimmy:** Go home? You were looking forward to this.

**Deirdre:** I was looking forward to walking into a normal house, not breaking into a mausoleum – and I

|  | don't like that Harry – he's an awful spoofer ... |
|---|---|
| **Jimmy:** | Hold on now, Harry is my friend. |
| **Deirdre:** | He is not, Jimmy. |
| **Jimmy:** | He is and so is Nick and Maurice and Paudge ... |
| **Deirdre:** | You haven't seen them for fifteen years. |
| **Jimmy:** | That doesn't matter: we were the Apaches – and once an Apache, always an Apache. |
| **Deirdre:** | Oh for God's sake! |
| **Jimmy:** | *(Angrily, as he dries himself)* And I know why you want to go: it's because you don't want me to have any friends – and you never did! |
| **Deirdre:** | I'd be delighted if you had friends, Jimmy. |
| **Jimmy:** | Then why are we always moving? |
| **Deirdre:** | What? |
| **Jimmy:** | Moving! Just as I start making friends in one place, you always want to move somewhere else. |
| **Deirdre:** | When did I want to move? Are you drunk already? |
| **Jimmy:** | Don't deny it – I had all my friends in Sallynoggin and as soon as you saw that, you wanted to move to Rathfarnham. |
| **Deirdre:** | And you can't make friends in Rathfarnham, can you not? Or what is it, I wonder, that the people of Sallynoggin have that makes them friendlier than the people of Rathfarnham? |
| **Jimmy:** | How do I know. |
| **Deirdre:** | Well I'll tell you: it's because the 'friends' you're talking about in Sallynoggin are all your own family: your mother, your sisters, your brothers and their wives – and I have no intention of moving back there! |
| **Jimmy:** | Right! – well we're not moving from here either and these are my oldest friends and I'm proud of them and we're going to stay here and enjoy this reunion, whether you bloody-well like it or not. *(Pause)* Did you tell Harry that you made meringues for this evening. |
| **Deirdre:** | No. |

| | |
|---|---|
| **Jimmy:** | Well do – that'll go down well. And if he asks you what I am ... |
| **Deirdre:** | I know – you're a little squirrel. |
| **Jimmy:** | I'm a pest control specialist! |
| **Deirdre:** | I told him that. |
| **Jimmy:** | And not a rat catcher! As far as they're concerned, I've nothing to do with rats. |
| **Deirdre:** | I said that once as a joke and you never forgot it. |
| **Jimmy:** | You said it in the front garden and the whole of Rathfarnham never forgot it! Did Harry tell you about his travel business? |
| **Deirdre:** | Yes and he gave me his card. I'll frame it when I get home. |
| **Jimmy:** | Just keep it safe. *(Looks around)* Hard to imagine: fifteen years ago we were sitting here doing our Leaving ... |
| **Deirdre:** | *(Sarcastic)* And tonight you're all coming back as mature men. |
| **Jimmy:** | Exactly. Now if you adopt that attitude, and join in, then we'll all enjoy ourselves. |
| | *(Harry comes in. He carries more six-packs)* |
| **Harry:** | *(Sees Jimmy)* Hey, Apache. *(Sings and stomps)* 'On the banks of the river ...' |
| **Jimmy:** | *(Joins in their recognised dance/stomp)* ... 'stood Running Bear, young Indian brave ...' Ah Crazy Horse *(To Deirdre)* that's his name, you know *(To Harry)* it's great to be back in the old Happy Hunting Ground. |
| **Harry:** | Sure is – but how did I miss you coming in, Little Beaver *(To Deirdre)* that was *his* name. |
| **Jimmy:** | No, Harry – Squirrel, Little Squirrel. |
| **Harry:** | What? |
| **Jimmy:** | I was Little Squirrel. |
| **Harry:** | Oh right – so did you come up the back stairs or what? |
| **Jimmy:** | Tell him Deirdre. |
| **Deirdre:** | He crawled up the drainpipe. |
| **Harry:** | What? |

| | |
|---|---|
| **Jimmy:** | I *climbed* up the drainpipe, just like in the old days, and in the window. |
| **Harry:** | *(To Deirdre)* Is he serious? |
| **Deirdre:** | *(Patiently)* Oh he is. |
| **Jimmy:** | Little Squirrel could do it then and he can still do it. |
| **Harry:** | Well fair dues – *(of his wet hair)* I thought someone had thrown a pint over you. |
| **Jimmy:** | *(Merrily)* No – that'll come later, eh? |
| **Harry:** | Now you've said it! Okay, let's get the place into some kind of order before the lads arrive. |
| | *(Jimmy and Harry will put out the desks, try to clean up the room, set out the bottles)* |
| **Jimmy:** | On their way, are they? |
| **Harry:** | Paudge still hadn't arrived at the pub – but Nick should be here – and I just saw Maurice down in the car-park. |
| **Jimmy:** | Still annoyed that we're not at his house, I suppose? |
| **Harry:** | Yeah, but worse – remember the cine camera he had at school? |
| **Jimmy:** | Jaysus yeah – Alfred Hitchcock. |
| **Harry:** | Well he thinks he'll be showing his shaggin' silent films here. |
| **Jimmy:** | Ah that's not on. |
| **Harry:** | It certainly is not and I'm going to tell him straight ... |
| **Jimmy:** | And I'll back you a hundred percent, Harry. |
| **Harry:** | A good piss-up is what we want here – not an old maids get-together. Put the bottles out here. |
| **Jimmy:** | We have a ton of stuff in the car. *(Stands back)* I wonder, Harry, if we've all changed much since we sat in those desks. |
| **Harry:** | You'll find we all done very well, Jimmy. |
| **Jimmy:** | Yeah – Deirdre says you gave her your business card – thanks a lot for that. |
| **Harry:** | No problem – and you're in pest control. |
| **Jimmy:** | I am – three vans on the road: it's all very sophis- |

ticated nowadays, Harry – we deal mainly in the eradication of Hymenoptera, Pica Rustica and, of course, the Larva of Anobium Punctatum.

**Harry:** That's terrific. And what are they?

**Jimmy:** Well. In layman's terms: ants, magpies and woodworm – basically any pest that can land or infiltrate anywhere. It's now a very scientific, sophisticated, full-time job.

**Harry:** Great. And do you do anything, Deirdre?

**Deirdre:** (*Coldly*) Yes, I make meringues.

**Jimmy:** No, Deirdre, you used to be a nurse.

**Deirdre:** Now I make meringues like his mother and his sisters in Sallynoggin.

**Jimmy:** (*Quickly*) And me and our three sons think they are delicious. Do you have a wife and kids yourself, Harry?

**Harry:** There might be kids but I don't know of any wife.

**Jimmy:** Then you don't know what you're missing – eh, Deirdre?

**Deirdre:** No.

**Harry:** Oh someday, in a weak moment, I'll walk into the trap.

**Jimmy:** We all do, Harry, we all do.

(*Maurice arrives at the door. He is tall, delicate and precise, looking older than his 32 years. He wears glasses. He has struggled up the stairs with a projector and a suitcase. He leaves the suitcase as he carries the projector in*)

**Maurice:** Ah gentlemen – sorry I'm late.

**Harry:** Come in, Maurice – Jimmy has arrived: came up the drainpipe.

**Maurice:** (*Stops*) Pardon me?

**Jimmy:** Just like in the old days, Tall Buffalo (*To Deirdre*) that's what we called him.

**Maurice:** (*To Deirdre*) Don't ask me why – Harry was Crazy Horse and I remember that you, Jimmy, were called Little Weasel.

**Jimmy:** No no, Squirrel – Little Squirrel.

**Maurice:** Squirrel?

**Harry:** So called because he used to climb the drainpipe.

**Maurice:** The drainpipe? I don't remember that now.

**Harry:** *(Laughs)* To tell you the truth, Maurice, neither do I.

**Jimmy:** Yes you do. *(To Deirdre)* They're desperate messers.

**Harry:** And you met Jimmy's lovely wife, Deirdre.

**Maurice:** Yes, briefly in the pub. Hello.

**Deirdre:** Hello again.

**Harry:** And Nick and Paudge are still as-lathar.

**Maurice:** Bad news, gentlemen – it seems Paudge will not be coming.

**Jimmy:** What?

**Harry:** Why not?

**Maurice:** Some farming trouble – he said if he wasn't in the pub by ten we could assume he wouldn't be here.

**Harry:** Ah Jaysus – I even left a note with the barman saying where we'd be.

**Maurice:** He was very sorry.

**Jimmy:** *(To Deirdre)* You'd've like him – really tough guy – now runs a farm in Tipperary.

**Maurice:** But Nick should have arrived by now.

**Jimmy:** He left the pub before us – remember, Deirdre, the one with the pony-tail.

**Deirdre:** Oh the fashion designer – he looks nice.

**Harry:** I'd keep and eye on her, Jimmy.

**Jimmy:** Don't worry, I will.
*(Maurice has carried in the packed suitcase)*

**Maurice:** Hopefully, gentlemen, we can get the party going at exactly midnight.

**Harry:** Excuse me, Maurice, but what exactly is all this stuff?

**Maurice:** My projector and a suitcase of films that will show us ourselves, as Dylan Thomas put it, when we 'were young and easy under the apple boughs and happy as the grass was green'.

**Harry:** With all due respects, Maurice, that is not the

kind of party we're having here tonight.

**Maurice:** With all due respects, Harry, it is.

**Harry:** I'm sorry, Maurice ...

**Maurice:** Harry, it is the same party we'd be having if we were having it in my house, where we were supposed to have it.

**Harry:** Except that we decided to have it here ...

**Maurice:** (*Angrily*) No, *you* decided, ignoring the fact that I had prepared everything at home ...

**Harry:** What's there to prepare? – we have all the booze here ...

**Maurice:** The projector was set-up in the house, there is food in the house – there are sandwiches, cocktail sausages, there is a fire lit ...

**Harry:** Ah for God's sake ...

**Maurice:** ... there is tea, there is coffee, there are vol-au-vents, there are cakes ...

**Harry:** Jaysus, it's not an old-folks reunion.

**Jimmy:** Deirdre brought some meringues – we have them in the car.

**Maurice:** That is not the point, Jimmy – we shouldn't be here.

**Harry:** Except that coming here was the democratic decision of all of us ...

**Maurice:** All of who? – we weren't all there ...

**Harry:** Okay, right, let's have a democratic decision by all of us here: who wants to go back to Maurice's house?

(*Deirdre puts up her hand*)

**Jimmy:** Deirdre!

(*She quickly takes it down*)

**Maurice:** (*Controlled*) Harry, are you just unwilling or are you too stupid to see my point?

**Harry:** (*Angrily*) I am not stupid, I was never stupid and there is no point!

**Maurice:** (*Sternly*) Of course there's a point: The point is that it was I, not you, who first thought of this reunion. It was I, not you, who contacted everybody. It was I, not you, who planned out this evening – and I have no intention of now allowing you to just walk in and turn what should be an evening of some interest into a stupid booze-up ...

**Harry:** Now you just hold on.

**Maurice:** *(Furiously)* ... because times have changed, Harry, and I'm no longer the young fellow who was great when you wanted the answers for the exams but could be laughed-at every other time. Don't you make the mistake of thinking I'm Gregory – that was all a long time ago and no one is going to be bullied by you now, least of all me!

**Harry:** Jesus, take it easy, will you.

**Maurice:** *(Calmer)* I have brought the projector and I have brought the films and I believe we should see them.

**Harry:** Then we'll see the shaggin' things if it saves you getting a nervous breakdown.

**Maurice:** *(Takes sheets of paper from the suitcase. Hands them out)* And there is also a programme I have set out. I suggest, if possible, we should follow it.

**Harry:** Does it include a game of hop-scotch?

**Maurice:** *(Pins a programme to the blackboard)* It will give the evening a sense of order from which we may derive some satisfaction and benefit. And I think I'll project to the back wall – and there's no power-point in here, so we'll see what's next door. I do want to start at exactly midnight. Thank you.

*(Maurice angrily takes the projector flex into the partition room)*

**Harry:** Jesus Christ, he's going to turn this into shaggin' night-school.

**Jimmy:** I always said he was too brainy.

**Harry:** Well I'd rather be thick. Do you know what his job is?

**Jimmy:** He was going to be a priest at school.

**Harry:**      He was booted out of that – now he sells insurance to people by telling them how easy it is to
get cancer or leukaemia or a brain haemorrhage
that would have blood pumping out of your ears.
Did you not hear him in the pub?

**Jimmy:**      Well we were sitting over at the ...

**Harry:**      He sounded like shaggin' Dracula: three fellows
beside him drank up and ran out of the place. I
warned you about him, Deirdre, didn't I?

**Deirdre:**    I thought he was nice.

**Harry:**      *(Hard)* Oh good – then you'll enjoy yourself anyway!

**Jimmy:**      *(To Deirdre)* Jesus!

**Harry:**      To think I was looking forward to this.

**Jimmy:**      It might pick up – he might have some good films
there.

**Harry:**      Yeah – like the Pope's visit to Ireland.

**Jimmy:**      Oh Jaysus, stop!

**Deirdre:**    But, Jimmy, you bought the video of the Pope's
visit to Ireland after we went up to the Phoenix
Park ...

**Jimmy:**      *(Quickly)* Deirdre, would you go down and get
your meringues.

**Deirdre:**    What?

**Jimmy:**      Here's the car-keys and take your umbrella –
we're starting at midnight.

**Deirdre:**    Nobody wants meringues ...

**Jimmy:**      *(Quietly)* Just get them – and stop answering back.

**Deirdre:**    *(Quietly)* Right, Little Weasel! *(Goes angrily)*

**Jimmy:**      *(Calls merrily)* I'll get our six-packs later – and
don't come up by the drainpipe. *(To Harry)* Only
Little Squirrel can do that, eh, Harry?
*(Harry is dialling on his cellular phone)*

**Harry:**      I'm not putting up with much more of this.

**Jimmy:**      Maurice?

**Harry:**      Or anyone else! I'm supposed to watch my blood
pressure and the last thing I need is that bastard
shouting at me.

| | |
|---|---|
| **Jimmy:** | Oh quite agree ... |
| **Harry:** | *(Annoyed, dials again)* And another thing, were you told you could bring a woman with you tonight? |
| **Jimmy:** | A woman? |
| **Harry:** | Because I shaggin' wasn't. |
| **Jimmy:** | You mean Deirdre? Jesus, was I not supposed ... ? |
| **Harry:** | I could've brought any one of a stack of women if I wanted to – and classy birds: models, air-hostesses, television presenters – only I thought we all agreed they'd only ruin the night. *(Into the phone)* Paul? Harry – what's the latest from Spain? *(Angrily)* Well find out! |
| **Jimmy:** | Harry, I'm terrible sorry about Deirdre ... |
| **Harry:** | *(To Jimmy)* Three charter flights in Barcelona and the airport is still closed. |
| **Jimmy:** | Will you have to fly out? |
| **Harry:** | *(Angrily to Jimmy)* The airport is closed! – I'm not one of your magpies – I can't land anywhere I like. *(Into phone)* Yes I'm here – go on. |
| | *(As Harry listens, Maurice comes from the room. He holds the plug. He will go to his suitcase, take out a tool kit and undo the plug)* |
| **Maurice:** | It's a three-pin socket – I'll have to bare the wires. |
| **Jimmy:** | Right. |
| **Maurice:** | And I really want to apologise to you all for my violent outburst just now. |
| **Jimmy:** | *(Quietly)* I think Harry would really like to hear you say that. |
| **Maurice:** | Yes and I will. How is he? |
| **Jimmy:** | On about the airport strike. *(Quietly)* Maurice, I'm sorry I brought Deirdre with me. |
| **Maurice:** | Oh I'm glad you did. I wish I had a wife to bring – but I'm resigned. Looking after my sick father is a full-time job anyway. |
| **Jimmy:** | Still alive, is he? |
| **Maurice:** | Only just and in his eighties – the doctor hardly bothers anymore ... and he got the Last Sacra- |

ments again on Friday. But then every time I
think this time he won't recover, he gets up, goes
into the front room and starts to play the piano.
Except that he's not really playing it – he's just
banging on the keys, but to him he's playing 'Oft
in the Stilly Night' that my mother used to sing.

**Harry:** *(Into the phone)* Let the shaggers sweat it out –
we're not providing any hotel.

**Maurice:** *(To Jimmy)* However, the good news is that I did
manage to get him an insurance policy that not
only covers his funeral expenses but also perpetual care of his grave. That cheered him up so much
that he started talking about learning to play the
accordion. They are a great investment, Jimmy –
you should think about getting one.

**Jimmy:** An accordion?

**Maurice:** No, an insurance policy.

**Harry:** *(Into the phone)* If anything changes, ring me.
Okay, Paul, ciao. *(Clicks off)*

**Jimmy:** Harry, I think Maurice wants to say something.

**Harry:** The only thing I want to hear from him is that that
projector is banjaxed and that we can get a proper
party going.

**Maurice:** *(Goes to Harry)* No, I just want to sincerely apolo-
gise, Harry, for losing control and for saying what
I said to you. I shouldn't have done it and I'm
very sorry and it won't happen again.

**Harry:** What? Oh right, well that's okay. And the projector isn't broken?

**Jimmy:** No, he's just fixing the plug.

**Harry:** Okay. *(Checks his watch)* Where the hell is Nick?

**Maurice:** And Harry, one more thing.

**Harry:** Yeah?

**Maurice:** You wouldn't mind if I used your telephone
sometime, would you?

**Harry:** What?

**Maurice:** Just to ring my father, to see how he is.

**Jimmy:** His father is dying though he still manages to

play the piano – 'Oft in the Stilly Night'.

**Harry:** And you want to start ringing him on my mobile during the night?

**Maurice:** Well he doesn't sleep when I'm out so he gets anxious and lonely.

**Harry:** *(Angrily)* Oh sure, I can't think of a better reason for having a mobile phone than for ringing the anxious and the lonely – do you want to start now?

**Maurice:** Well maybe later, if that's all right.

**Harry:** Sure, anytime you like, tell him a bedtime story on it if you want.

**Maurice:** Thanks Harry, that's a good idea, I will. And sorry for my outburst, won't happen again. *(Looks at his watch)* And as we've only fifteen minutes to go to starting time, as per our programme, I think I'll put the bare wires into the socket direct. *(Goes)*

**Harry:** I know where he should put the bare wires – do us all a favour.

**Jimmy:** He's worried how it'll all go.

**Harry:** *(Looking at the pin-up programme)* So he should with this crap. *(Reads)* 'Item One – Introductions: meet the old tribe. Two. At midnight. A personal retrospective by each Apache. Three. A cinematic stroll down memory lane.' Well he can shove that – I'll be taking a stroll home if Nick isn't here soon.

**Jimmy:** Yeah. Agreed.

**Harry:** And then asking for my mobile.

**Jimmy:** Jaysas that took some nerve.

**Harry:** A riot in Barcelona and Paul in the office can't reach me because he's talking to his lonely father. He's out to ruin this night for everyone.

*(Nick appears at the door. He is 32, well-dressed in casuals, his hair in a pony-tail, he carries a bottle of wine and two glasses. He is very assured. He smokes)*

**Nick:** My fellow Apaches – Running Bear has arrived.

**Harry:** Jaysas, where have you been?

**Nick:**     *(Sings and stomps)* 'On the banks of the river, stood Running Bear, young Indian brave ...'

**Harry:**   *(Anxiously)* Nick, we've problems – what the hell kept you?

**Nick:**     I was looking around – isn't this place really amazing? I mean lights everywhere, desks still in the classrooms, stuff still in the science laboratory – and look at this ... this is the concept of a lifetime.

**Harry:**   Nick ... ?

**Nick:**     You know, I could do something really amazingly creative in a place like this – A fashion show I could call 'Style Amongst the Squalor'.

**Harry:**   Jaysas, will you forget your job for one minute and listen.

**Nick:**     And hello again, Jimmy – or should I say Little Squirrel.

**Jimmy:**   You remembered my name!

**Nick:**     Course I did – Little Squirrel always climbing the drainpipe and up and down every tree in the woods.

**Jimmy:**   *(To Harry)* See? He remembers it all.

**Harry:**   How do you remember all that?

**Nick:**     I don't – I met his wife in the car-park and she told me.

**Harry:**   *(Laughs)* I was wondering.

**Jimmy:**   You were talking to Deirdre?

**Nick:**     Sorry Jimmy, but I probably would have remembered anyway – but I remember that window.

**Harry:**   Jaysas, don't we all.

**Nick:**     *(Looking up)* Wonder if they're still up there?

**Jimmy:**   What?

**Nick:**     Were you not there the day we put up our names?

**Jimmy:**   *(Recovers)* Oh yeah, our names – Jaysas I remember that all right.

**Nick:**     This is going to be an amazing night – there's more booze below in the car ...

**Harry:**   Except that we have a few problems – like you

|  | heard Paudge can't make it? |
|---|---|
| **Nick:** | Maurice said that in the pub – that's okay, we can live without Chief Sitting Bull-shit. |
| **Jimmy:** | *(Laughs)* Oh, we'd never say that to his face. |
| **Harry:** | Okay – but there's something worse – there's Maurice – look, he brought his shaggin' projector ... |
| **Jimmy:** | He's in there wiring up the shaggin' plug. |
| **Nick:** | Yeah, your Deirdre was telling me – but that's okay isn't it? |
| **Harry:** | What? Yeah well, that's okay in itself, I suppose – but just look at the programme he's set out for the whole evening. |
| **Nick:** | Is it all about insurance policies and terminal cancer? |
| **Harry:** | It's nearly as depressing – take a look and prepare to shaggin' weep. |
| **Nick:** | *(Reading)* 'Item One. Introductions – meet the old tribe.' Well that's okay, we did that. 'Item Two. At midnight. A personal retrospective by each Apache.' That's good, there could be a few laughs there. |
| **Harry:** | *(Backing down)* Well yeah, that's good all right ... |
| **Nick:** | *(Reading)* 'Item three – a cinematic stroll down memory lane ...' |
| **Harry:** | On his silent films! |
| **Nick:** | Sure – but we don't have to stay silent, do we – could be great slaggin' at the bygone days. |
| **Harry:** | *(Backing down)* Oh well yeah, that's a point I suppose ... |
| **Jimmy:** | It's a good point, Harry. |
| **Nick:** | At least it's not a God-awful boring video ... |
| **Harry:** | Oh agreed – but it's so ... organised ... |
| **Nick:** | Sure, but we don't want a mindless piss-up do we? |
| **Harry:** | Jaysas no – nobody wants that. |
| **Jimmy:** | Last thing in the world we want ... |
| **Nick:** | Then that all sounds very good indeed, as a |

general plan.

**Harry:** *(Annoyed)* Well as long as we're all happy with it.

**Nick:** Well I am.

**Jimmy:** Me too. And I think Deirdre was.

**Nick:** Your Deirdre was very enthusiastic about it.

**Harry:** *(Coldly)* Oh she was, was she.

**Jimmy:** And where is she now – Deirdre?

**Nick:** I left her talking to Jackie.

**Jimmy:** Jackie? Who's he?

**Nick:** Jackie, my wife. *(To Harry)* Soon as I heard Paudge wasn't coming, I went home and got her. Good move, eh?

**Harry:** *(Not happy)* You have her here with you?

**Nick:** Sure have. *(To Jimmy)* You remember Jackie Sutton from Sacred Heart Convent – she was nearly one of the gang.

**Harry:** *(Coldly to Jimmy)* Her name was Jacinta then.

**Jimmy:** Oh her – but wasn't she going out with Paudge?

**Nick:** Ancient history, Jimmy – and folks, speak of an angel ...

*(Jackie Sutton comes in. She is 30, assured, fashionably dressed. She carries a bottle of wine – and is eating something)*

**Jackie:** Darling, this place must be like a lighthouse to every police car.

**Nick:** It's all right, we're at the back of the school – are you eating something, darling?

**Jackie:** A meringue – if you're Jimmy, these are your wife's and they are delicious.

**Jimmy:** Oh hello – yes – great. Where exactly is she?

**Jackie:** On her way up, turning off lights – telling me how spooky this room is.

**Nick:** *(Lightly)* How could a classroom be spooky! You remember Harry Lawless, darling?

**Jackie:** Well of course. The Globe Trotter. *(Shakes hands)* Is your travel business affected by this Spanish strike?

**Harry:** *(Coldly)* Not really, Jacinta – nothing we haven't handled before.

**Nick:** Harry – it's Jackie now.

**Jackie:** It's been Jackie a long time.

*(Maurice comes from the partition room)*

**Maurice:** Nick! I thought I heard you.

**Nick:** Hello Maurice – you remember Jackie Sutton?

**Maurice:** *(Lost)* Pardon?

**Nick:** *(Then)* Jacinta Sutton?

**Maurice:** Oh Jacinta – of course I do.

**Jackie:** It's Jackie now – lovely to see you again, Maurice.

**Maurice:** You're the one that when all the other girls were wearing their grey school berets, you always had a big straw hat.

**Jackie:** Yes!

**Harry:** *(Disgusted)* Jesus Christ!

**Maurice:** Always tied with pink ribbon.

**Jackie:** How wonderful of you to remember that, Maurice.

**Nick:** I think that's amazing – because I don't even remember it!

**Jackie:** I won't let that spoil my evening. *(Kisses Nick)*

**Maurice:** Now, only five minutes to go, everybody. Perhaps we'll lift the projector up on this table?

*(Jimmy will help Maurice to set the projector in place – after which Maurice will find some chalk and transfer the programme onto the blackboard)*

**Harry:** *(Coldly)* So what have you been doing, Jackie – since you stopped wearing straw hats?

**Jackie:** Married Nick, one little girl, Emma, what else ... ?

**Harry:** No, like work.

**Jackie:** Oh, I'm in the rag trade actually.

**Nick:** You know the fashion shop 'Style-Line' in Wicklow Street and Henry Street?

**Harry:** Yeah, that's pretty high-class – a girlfriend of mine shops there all the time ... in the Wicklow Street one.

**Nick:** That's where Jackie is.

**Jimmy:** Oh great – which one and I'll get Deirdre to go in and say hello.

**Harry:** If it's the lingerie department, he'll go in himself.

**Jackie:** Well I'm not actually in any of them.

**Nick:** She owns them – and a new one opening in Cork.

**Jimmy:** You own them?

**Harry:** *(Amused)* Is ... is this a joke?

**Nick:** No, six years ago she had this amazing plan ...

**Jackie:** ... and some good friends and a lot of neck and a very sympathetic bank manager ... and so far, so good.

**Jimmy:** *(Taken aback)* Well, that's great.

**Harry:** *(Quietly angry)* Yeah ... that's ... terrific.

**Maurice:** Now, is everybody familiar with our programme?

**Nick:** *(To Jackie)* Over there, love – It's wonderful.

*(Jackie goes to where Maurice is writing the programme onto the blackboard. Deirdre comes in. She carries a cake tin and a large carton of beer glasses and her umbrella)*

**Deirdre:** Jimmy, I shouldn't have turned off all the lights because you still have to get your drink.

**Jimmy:** Don't worry. I understand you met Nick ...

**Deirdre:** Oh yes – and I also found out that Jackie was one year behind me in Sacred Heart.

**Nick:** Did you know each other?

**Jackie:** No, but I knew Deirdre's sister ...

**Deirdre:** Cecily.

**Jackie:** And I always knew that Cecily's sister was mad about nursing.

**Deirdre:** And that was me.

**Maurice:** You're a nurse, Deirdre?

**Deirdre:** Well I was until ...

**Jackie:** It's an incredible story: one day Jimmy came to their family house to catch this huge rat that was running around ...

**Jimmy:** Excuse me Jackie, where did you hear this?

**Jackie:** Deirdre told me ...

**Deirdre:** It's all right, Jimmy ...

**Jimmy:** It's not all right because first of all it wasn't a rat

...

**Deirdre:** I didn't say it was definitely a rat.

**Jackie:** And it doesn't really matter – Jimmy came to catch a rat and while he was catching it, Deirdre couldn't take her eyes off him ...

**Harry:** Well yeah, compared to a rat, Jimmy does look good.

*(Laughter)*

**Jimmy:** *(Angrily to Deirdre)* Satisfied now?

**Jackie:** And her mother said to Deirdre: 'Just because that fellow catches the rat doesn't mean he can catch you too ...'

**Deirdre:** And I was raging but then suddenly didn't Jimmy grab the rat and, as he did, he fell off the ladder and broke his arm and the rat escaped and bit my mother.

**Jimmy:** Deirdre, would you ever ... !

**Jackie:** And romance blossomed as Deirdre the Nurse attended to him but because of the bite, her mother never came to their wedding ...

**Jimmy:** *(Furious to Deirdre)* That wasn't the reason your mother ...

**Deirdre:** No, that was more because *your* mother wanted me to give up nursing once we got married ...

**Jimmy:** You wanted to give it up, Deirdre.

**Deirdre:** Jimmy ...

**Jimmy:** *(Furious)* And I really think we should shut up about this now?!

**Jackie:** No, it's a wonderful story – because, at the wedding breakfast ...

**Maurice:** Indeed, Jackie – but now our festivities are almost ready to begin ...

**Jimmy:** Exactly – and anyway what we're hearing is not what we're here to hear!

**Maurice:** So now, with time running out, with our introductions over and before the second item on our programme – the Apaches' individual retrospectives – I suggest that the young braves should get

up any food and fire-water that they may need,
while the ladies and I put the finishing touches to
the room.

**Harry:** Right – the booze – let's go Apaches!

**Nick:** Yes, come on, War party. 'On the banks of the
river ...' (*Goes*)

**Harry:** (*Going*) Right with you, Running Bear ...

**Maurice:** And Harry, may I borrow your telephone now?

**Harry:** What? Oh right. (*Gives it to him*) Come on, Little
Squirrel. (*Goes*)
(*Nick and Harry can be heard singing 'on the banks of
the river'. Jimmy goes to Deirdre*)

**Jimmy:** Can you not keep your mouth shut?

**Deirdre:** You told me to join in.

**Jimmy:** Well now would you ever join *out* – and shut-up
about me and rats and running around telling
Nick I was called Little Squirrel.

**Deirdre:** I only told him because ...

**Harry:** (*Off*) Jimmy!

**Jimmy:** (*To Deirdre*) Well you didn't need to – he remembered – he's not a fool, he's an intelligent man.
(*Shouts*) Coming, Crazy Horse. (*Goes*)

**Maurice:** Best if we put the desks here.

**Jackie:** Wonderful – this is going to be a wonderful evening, you were great to think it up.

**Maurice:** I've been planning it for a long time, Jackie.

**Deirdre:** (*Helping*) Jimmy has been talking about nothing
else for weeks.

**Jackie:** Nick remembering the names of everyone.

**Maurice:** And did they ever mention Gregory?

**Jackie:** Gregory? No, who was he?

**Maurice:** Just one of the lads.

**Deirdre:** Now there's something – Jimmy was trying to
catch a Gregory once – I mean, when Jimmy is out
working, trying to catch something, a mouse or
whatever, he gives them a name – turns it into a
war between him and them ...

**Jackie:** That's a wonderful idea.

**Deirdre:** Once he was going after a swarm of wasps and he called them 'The Mormon Tabernacle Choir'.

**Jackie:** *(To Maurice)* She has marvellous stories.

**Deirdre:** But, about Gregory – I remember that soon after we got married, Jimmy used to wake up in the middle of the night shouting out 'Gregory Gregory' and I used to ask him what was Gregory and eventually he told me it was a mouse he was after and I remember saying to him that I wish to God he'd catch it because I can't get a wink of sleep.

**Jackie:** Really?

**Maurice:** And does he still call it out?

**Deirdre:** Ah no, it stopped – I think he must have eventually killed Gregory.

**Maurice:** Right. Now, there's another desk in this room – would you help me carry it in, Deirdre.

**Deirdre:** As long as there's no spiders in there – I can't stand them ... but don't tell Jimmy!

**Maurice:** I won't – just mind the flex. Then I'll phone my father.

*(Maurice and Deirdre go into the room. Jackie is working on when Paudge appears at the door. He is 32, big and quiet: his size almost speaks for him. He wears a suit. His accent is rural. He carries a six-pack)*

**Paudge:** Jackie?

**Jackie:** *(Looks)* Oh Christ!

**Paudge:** *(Smiles)* No it's Paudge actually.

**Jackie:** But you weren't supposed ... Nick said ... have you seen Nick?

**Paudge:** In the car-park – but he didn't see me. *(Moves towards her)* I wanted a chance to see you first.

**Jackie:** *(Adamant)* Oh no – sorry, no, Paudge. *(Calls)* Maurice, look who's here – Paudge has arrived.

**Paudge:** *(Annoyed)* Thanks, Jackie.

*(Maurice appears)*

**Maurice:** Well what a surprise – you're just in time, Chief Sitting Bull.

(Blackout)

END OF SCENE ONE, ACT ONE

# ACT ONE
# SCENE TWO

*Twenty minutes later. The storm continues outside. The projector is in position. Some desks have become the 'bar': laden with bottles and cans. Deirdre's cake tin here also.*

*A 'classroom' ritual seems to be in place – all desks facing a top table, where Nick stands. The atmosphere is boisterous: Harry, Jimmy, Paudge sitting in the desks, Drinking/Smoking/Heckling. Jackie and Deirdre sitting at the back, enjoying it all.*

*Maurice stands to the side of Nick, who is trying to finish his individual retrospective.*

*The scene opens in a barrage of noise, with Maurice trying to quieten it down.*

| | |
|---|---|
| **Nick:** | ... It is all of those things that bring back the memory to me tonight ... |
| **Harry:** | *(Throwing beer at Jimmy)* Hey Jimmy, is that rain getting in? |
| **Jimmy:** | *(Enjoying it)* Mess off, Harry. |
| **Jackie:** | Nick is speaking. |
| **Harry:** | I done nothing. *(Throws drink again)* There it is again. |
| **Jimmy:** | Paudge, defend me here. |
| **Paudge:** | Leave me out of it. |
| **Maurice:** | Gentlemen! |
| **Harry:** | I'm doing nothing. |
| **Jimmy:** | *(To Harry)* Do it to Paudge. |
| **Maurice:** | *(Loudly)* Please gentlemen, please! *(A quietness)* Carry on, Nick. |
| **Nick:** | And now, my fellow Apaches, I would like to end by saying ... |
| **Harry:** | And about time too. |
| **Jackie:** | Quiet, Harry. |
| **Harry:** | I only got five minutes for my individual retrospective – he's been up there for ten. |

**Jackie:** Maybe he has more to say.

**Jimmy:** I only got three ...

**Nick:** *(Trying)* I would like to end by saying ...

**Harry:** You were very good on the woodworm, Jimmy.

**Deirdre:** Yes, very good, Jimmy.

**Harry:** Especially their mating habits – you oul ram.

**Maurice:** Gentlemen, please! – we must let Nick end because Paudge is waiting.

**Paudge:** Ah I'll be no good at this talking.

**Jimmy:** Actions, eh, Paudge?

**Nick:** I would like to end by saying that, looking back, I've had the most amazing good fortune, always had Lady Luck on my side ...

**Harry:** Ya Ram!

**Nick:** ... in going from this school to London to the College of Design, later to meet my darling Jackie who gave me so much support ...

**Jackie:** Thank you, darling.

**Harry:** *(Merrily)* You're next, Paudge.

**Nick:** ... to eventually my present position. And, in conclusion, I must register my appreciation to Maurice for his initiative in assembling all the old Apaches, for the first time since we left school, in this amazing old classroom ...

**Harry:** Excuse me!

**Nick:** *(Corrects)* ... which was Harry's idea – weeks before it will disappear forever ...

**Maurice:** And we did all meet once before, Nick, at a funeral.

**Nick:** Okay. And so, in keeping with the previous speakers – Harry, Jimmy and Maurice – I reiterate: this is a night I expect to remember forever. Thank you.

*(A Cheer. Nick goes to his desk)*

**Maurice:** Thank you, Nick. And now ...

**Jackie:** Maurice, are the ladies not allowed to have a retrospective?

**Maurice:** I'm afraid it's Apaches only, Jacinta.

Jackie:     Jackie!

Harry:      Anyway, we heard all about you and your shops.

Jackie:     I was thinking of Deirdre.

Jimmy:      Deirdre never gets up, Jackie – even at family parties.

Deirdre:    *(Quietly to Jackie)* His family parties!

Maurice:    Maybe we'll have you after the Apaches and the film, Jacint ... *(Corrects)* Jackie.

Harry:      *(Chants)* We want Paudge ... We want Paudge ...

Maurice:    But now, finally, we have the retrospective of our one and only chief – Chief Sitting Bull. Come on, Paudge.

Harry:      *(Cheers)* From the Apache's Tipperary branch.

Paudge:     *(Going to the table)* This will be very short.

Harry:      Give 'em hell. *(Drinks)*

Jackie:     *(To Deirdre)* You're right – they have got very mature.

Maurice:    And then we will have the films. Go ahead, Paudge – quiet.
            *(A quietness. Some lightning)*

Paudge:     Fellow Apaches, first of all I can't believe I'm back here ... *(Loudly)* back in this old school: the Apaches' Happy Hunting Ground!
            *(A great cheer. Harry, Jimmy and Nick begin to sing and beat-out 'on the banks of the river ...')*

Maurice:    Please gentlemen. No singing – singing is item five on the programme.
            *(The singing continues. Then Harry suddenly stops)*

Harry:      *(Louder)* Everyone! Quiet – please! Quiet – lads! Lads!
            *(All stop. Harry has taken his cellular phone from his pocket. It is ringing)*

Harry:      This could be important – quiet now ... this could be from Spain.

Nick:       Jesus, someone wants their money back.

Jimmy:      They all want their money back.

Harry:      *(Sternly)* No, seriously now, no messing.

Maurice:    Yes gentlemen, quiet now.

**Harry:** *(Very affected into the phone)* Hello, Sun-Kissed Holidays, can I help you?

**Jackie:** Yes – give us a kiss.

**Harry:** *(Furiously to Jackie)* Will you shut-up. *(Into phone)* Would you mind speaking up please.

**Maurice:** Just have to wait a minute, Paudge.

**Paudge:** That's all right. *(Drinks)*

**Harry:** *(Into phone)* Oh you're at home – well what holiday were you on when you fell – was it in Spain or in Portugal?

**Nick:** Oh Jesus, compensation.

**Jimmy:** Could be millions.

**Harry:** *(Suddenly)* Jesus Christ! *(Angrily into phone)* No, I'm not Maurice. *(To Maurice)* Did you give your oul fella this number?

**Maurice:** Oh sorry, Harry – I said only if he had to. *(Into phone)* Hello daddy.

**Harry:** *(Furious)* Shaggin' phone tied up now – what does he think he's at?

**Maurice:** *(Into phone)* Daddy, that was only Harry.

**Harry:** *(To Maurice)* Who only owns the shaggin' phone – who's only trying to run a business from it!

**Jackie:** Did he say he's fallen?

**Harry:** *(Angrily)* I don't know and I don't care!

**Deirdre:** But he's an old-age pensioner.

**Harry:** And I'm a young-age businessman!

**Maurice:** *(Into the phone)* You shouldn't be in there, daddy – you should be in bed.

**Harry:** I wouldn't even make a personal call myself.

**Jackie:** Oh for God's sake, don't go on.

**Harry:** And neither would you from your famous shops – you and your *(Imitates)* 'very sympathetic bank manager'.

**Jackie:** Don't be so stupid.

**Harry:** I'm not stupid – there's nothing stupid about it – that happens to be a strictly commercial phone, not the Old Folks Hot Line.

**Jackie:** Yes, I remember you at school.

| | |
|---|---|
| **Harry:** | Christ, I remember you too! |
| **Nick:** | Knock it off, Harry. |
| **Harry:** | Tell her to knock it off. |
| **Maurice:** | *(Into phone)* No, leave the piano alone, daddy. |
| **Harry:** | *(To Jackie)* You weren't even invited here in the first place – either of you. |
| **Jackie:** | *(Hard)* Well, tough. |
| **Nick:** | *(Hard)* Stop it, Jackie. |
| **Jimmy:** | *(Pause. Then anxiously)* Deirdre, give out the meringues. |
| **Deirdre:** | What? |
| **Jimmy:** | *(Angrily)* Do something! Give out the meringues! |
| **Deirdre:** | Jesus! *(Opens the tin)* Meringues if anyone wants one. |
| **Jackie:** | Why not. *(Takes one)* |
| **Maurice:** | *(Into phone)* No, You can't play the piano for mammy because mammy can't hear you anymore. |
| **Harry:** | First his crappy programme and now a shaggin' oul fella that thinks he's Richard Clayderman. |
| **Maurice:** | *(Into phone)* That's right, daddy, because she's dead and now you go back to bed and read your Insurance Policies and don't be worrying. |
| **Nick:** | *(To Jackie)* I think he's okay. |
| **Harry:** | Of course he's okay but my blood pressure is far from okay. *(Takes some tablets)* |
| **Maurice:** | *(Into phone)* And you just phone me here if anything happens. Bye bye daddy. *(Clicks off the phone)* |
| **Jackie:** | Is he all right? |
| **Maurice:** | Oh yes – just slipped trying to open the piano. |
| **Jackie:** | Oh dear. |
| **Maurice:** | I always lock it going out – the neighbours get frightened when he starts to bang it. Thanks Harry. *(Gives him back the phone)* You didn't mind too much, did you? |
| **Harry:** | Oh no. I suppose you'll be ringing him again once he gets back into bed? |

**Maurice:** No, I'll leave him for a while now.

**Harry:** You'd want to mind he doesn't fall asleep.

**Paudge:** Are we ready now?

**Maurice:** I think so, Paudge. All right everybody, let us now proceed with our final Apache retrospective from our great Chief Sitting Bull.

*(A cheer)*

**Paudge:** Well, as I was saying, it's great to be here ... and I'll have to warn you, I'm not very good at this, I won't be as articulate as the rest of you, it's not what I'd volunteer to do ...

**Jimmy:** One man's meat, Paudge.

**Maurice:** Very true, Jimmy.

**Paudge:** ... and especially after hearing how well you've all done in your own individual occupations ...

**Jimmy:** One man's meat, Paudge, one man's meat.

**Harry:** *(Angrily)* Is there a shaggin' parrot in this room?

**Maurice:** Harry! Go on, Paudge.

**Paudge:** ... hearing about Maurice with his insurance, Harry with his travel business, Nick with his name in the papers ...

**Deirdre:** And his photograph ...

**Paudge:** True – Jimmy with his scientific pest control, Deirdre with her ... her ... *(Lost. Then)* who made the lovely meringues ...

**Deirdre:** That's me.

**Jackie:** She's a state registered nurse, for God's sake.

**Jimmy:** She is, Paudge – she still has the uniform at home.

**Paudge:** Fair enough – and then, of course, we come to my old friend of many years ago: Jackie.

**Harry:** *(Quietly)* Christ.

**Maurice:** Bygones be bygones, Paudge.

*(Uncomfortable silence)*

**Paudge:** Okay. *(Then)* And that, in a way, brings us to me. And I suppose we all wonder sometimes what other people really think of us and it's usually not what we think they think – and I sometimes wonder what all of you ever really thought of me.

**Maurice:**  Well first of all, you were our chief.

**Harry:**  I know what that fellow in Clongowes thought of you when you tackled him – I can still hear his leg going.

**Jimmy:**  Jaysas yeah – snap! He thought you were a stampeding rhinoceros.

**Deirdre:**  Jimmy always spoke very highly of you, Paudge.

**Paudge:**  *(Continuing)* And sometimes, all we have to go on is, not remembering what was said to our face, but what we heard when people thought we weren't there. And I remember one day, in sixth year, when I was coming back early to this very classroom, to get a Latin cog from you, Maurice ...

**Maurice:**  Always welcome, Paudge.

**Paudge:**  ... and just outside that very door, I stopped because I suddenly heard my name mentioned. Some fellow in here was saying how I was always talking about my mother and father on the farm in Tipperary but nobody ever saw them – and then another fellow said that maybe I didn't have a mother and father at all and that maybe Big Paudge wasn't just Big Paudge, he was really a Big Bastard.

**Harry:**  *(Uneasily)* I don't honestly remember anyone who ever ... said that.

**Paudge:**  And that got a great laugh – they were all standing there – and then another fellow added, to get an ever bigger laugh, that if all I was telling was lies, then maybe I should no longer be called Chief Sitting Bull, but Chief Sitting Bull-shit. *(Awkward silence)*

**Jimmy:**  *(Nervously)* I don't think anyone here ever said that.

**Harry:**  Certainly not to my knowledge.

**Maurice:**  Of course not, because we all knew your parents sent you up here where you lived with your aunt because this was a good school and you wanted to go on and become a vet.

**Deirdre:** Oh really? And did you become a vet, Paudge – I mean, are you one now?

**Jimmy:** *(Quietly)* Will you stop butting in.

**Paudge:** No, I am not, Deirdre! Big Paudge turned out to be exactly what he never wanted to be: a farmer running the family farm with about as much independence as the bull that we keep locked up out in the shed.

**Harry:** Paudge, we can't all be what we want to be.

**Maurice:** I wanted to be a priest – Nick wanted to be a scientist ...

**Jackie:** I never knew that.

**Nick:** *(Quietly)* It was only a phase ...

**Jimmy:** No, Nick was never out of the science laboratory ...

**Deirdre:** I wanted to go on to do osteopathics ...

**Harry:** *(Lightly)* I always wanted to run a high-class brothel!

**Maurice:** So Paudge, did you confront that straight on, what you heard – did you come in here and demand who said it?

**Paudge:** No.

**Maurice:** A mistake, Paudge, a mistake.

**Paudge:** *(Suddenly flings down his beer-can in fury)* I know – because I should have just kicked in the door, charged in and laid every bastard out and then smashed up every stick of furniture in this poxy room. But I let my chance go by – and not for the first time – and I walked over to the woods and sat there, remembering what I was being called.

**Harry:** *(Then)* Jaysas, Paudge, they were bastards, whoever they were – but remember we were all called something behind out backs ...

**Jimmy:** Even the teachers – Brother Holmes, the bastard, was called Sherlock ...

**Harry:** Mr Conroy was called Einstein ...

**Maurice:** I was called Alfred Hitchcock ...

**Deirdre:** And anyway, Paudge, it wasn't anyone here that

called you Chief Sitting Bull-sh ... *(Stops)* Called you that name, was it?

**Jimmy:** *(Quietly, furious to her)* Of all the questions to ask!

**Paudge:** *(Pause. Now calmly and pleasantly)* You're absolutely right, Deirdre – and that's what I decided eventually because, after all, you all called me The Chief to my face and you all knew what I'd do if I heard any of you calling me anything else behind my back.

**Maurice:** Exactly – because Deirdre *is* right: it could not have been an Apache.

**Harry:** Exactly.

**Jimmy:** Absolutely – quite right, Deirdre.

**Paudge:** And because of that, I'm glad I came – even though you all did better than me, I'm still glad to see you all again and I'm looking forward to the programme and especially the old films and to having a few drinks. Thank you.

*(A cheer as Paudge goes to his desk and Maurice assumes the top table again)*

**Harry:** *(Loudly)* And we're all glad you came, Paudge, and so, lads, get the party going, let's hear it for the Chief.

**Harry/Jimmy:** *(Performing the Apache stomp)* 'On the banks of the river, stood Running Bear young Indian brave. On the other side of the river, stood his lovely Indian maid ...'

*(As Harry and Jimmy dance, Maurice tries to gently gesticulate for them to stop. They continue)*

**Maurice:** *(Shouts)* Stop it!

*(They stop)*

**Maurice:** *(More controlled)* Singing is number five on the programme.

**Harry:** For Jaysas sake, is blowing our noses on the programme?

**Maurice:** No, Harry, it is best if we keep to the order – but I do suggest, before our film, that we register our disappointment in hearing that Paudge nearly

|          | didn't come ... |
| Deirdre: | Well yes .... |
| Maurice: | ... and if he feels that his life has been less than ideal, let me suggest that he is judging us as being successful ... |
| Harry:   | And we are. |
| Maurice: | ... without realising how successful he is himself. |
| Harry:   | Exactly. |
| Jimmy:   | I'd say that anything that Paudge would turn his hand to ... |
| Harry:   | Or his fist! |
| Jimmy:   | ... would be a success. |
| Maurice: | Precisely – so, Paudge, to illustrate this, let me ask you: how big is this farm of yours? |
| Paudge:  | The farm? |
| Maurice: | No false modesty now – how many acres is it? |
| Paudge:  | It's just the family farm and when my father died I had to go back and ... |
| Harry:   | Number of acres, Paudge? |
| Paudge:  | About two hundred. |
| Jimmy:   | Two hundred! |
| Harry:   | That's the size of an Indian reservation. |
| Jimmy:   | And how many cows and things on it? |
| Paudge:  | We've mixed farming – oh I do very well ... |
| Harry:   | And what kind of a car do you drive, Paudge? |
| Paudge:  | Car? Well, I've a Mercedes now ... |
| Deirdre: | A Mercedes! |
| Jimmy:   | This year's registration, I suppose? |
| Paudge:  | Well yes, but before that ... |
| Harry:   | And I bet you have one big ranchero on that reservation of yours ... |
| Paudge:  | It's a bungalow-type ... |
| Harry:   | Southfork! |
| Deirdre: | And are you married, Paudge? |
| Paudge:  | Oh I'm in no hurry. |
| Harry:   | Too many after you – ya oul ram! |
| Jimmy:   | Wanting to move in and hang up their hats. |
| Paudge:  | I won't say you're wrong there! |

**Maurice:**  See? Listen to what you're saying ...

**Jimmy:**  You're ahead of us all.

**Maurice:**  Professionally, you'd pass my insurance questionnaire every time – total success.

**Harry:**  And a whole lot better than the teachers in this very classroom who said we'd all end up emptying dustbins.

**Deirdre:**  What?

**Jackie:**  Who said that?

**Jimmy:**  No one said it.

**Harry:**  Brother Holmes said it, standing right there.

**Nick:**  No no, Harry ...

**Harry:**  Yes – the Apaches were made to sit in a block over there and Holmes would say to the whole class 'Look at the five bright sparks – in ten years time they'll be emptying your dustbins'.

**Jimmy:**  I don't remember that.

**Nick:**  Never happened.

**Maurice:**  But Harry's point is a good one: once you confront it, you can see how we all turned out – better than any of them.

**Harry:**  I passed Holmes in my BMW the other day and he looks like a shaggin' dustbin himself.

**Jimmy:**  And, Paudge, that all proves you're still top man – ahead of the best.
*(Jimmy raises a glass. All drink to Paudge)*

**Paudge:**  I appreciate that ... everyone. *(Drinks)*

**Maurice:**  Excellent – and now with that cleared up, we can move on to item number three on our programme – the showing of my old movies.

**Deirdre:**  Oh great.

**Paudge:**  Looking forward to this.

**Maurice:**  *(Light-hearted)* So perhaps the Indian Braves would move their tee-pees and the squaws would help move the chairs into position for the film ...
*(All help move the desks from the classroom setting and set the chairs in a row, beside the projector, facing the back-wall)*

**Harry:** *(Helping)* Where's the popcorn.

**Jimmy:** *(Helping)* Deirdre and I want the back row – this'll be like old times, Deirdre.

**Jackie:** Maurice, before the film begins, is it too much to hope for a loo?

**Deirdre:** Oh yes, me too.

**Harry:** Back of the bicycle shed.

**Maurice:** Certainly not – come with me, ladies – I'll find one for you.

**Deirdre:** Thanks Maurice – *(Lightly)* we wouldn't like going on our own with all the darkness and the lightning and the shadows everywhere.

**Jackie:** *(Lightly)* Deirdre, stop please!

**Maurice:** Nothing to worry about, ladies.

**Deirdre:** Don't show any films till we get back.

**Jimmy:** You're not in them, Deirdre.

**Deirdre:** *(Lightly)* I know – but you are!
*(Maurice, Deirdre and Jackie go)*

**Jimmy:** *(Lightly imitates Deirdre)* 'I know – but you are'.

**Harry:** Maurice has turned into a right oul wan.

**Paudge:** Maurice is all right.

**Harry:** *(Then)* Hey Jimmy, while we're waiting, why don't you climb up and see if our names are still over the window.

**Jimmy:** Great idea. Little Squirrel rides again.

**Harry:** Leave your sex life out of it. Pile the tables up ... it was over in that corner.

**Jimmy:** Before Maurice comes back.
*(From now, Harry and Jimmy will disturb the tables/chairs/desks to pile one on one)*

**Harry:** You sure you can manage this?

**Jimmy:** No trouble. You just hold them.
*(Harry hold the tables, as Jimmy begins to climb. Paudge has come to where Nick stands)*

**Paudge:** Jackie's looking well.

**Nick:** Jackie is great.

**Paudge:** And Emma – how is Emma?

**Nick:** Emma is fine, Paudge, fine.

| | |
|---|---|
| **Paudge:** | And are there further little brothers or sisters for her? |
| **Nick:** | *(Controlled)* A warning, Paudge – I'm not putting up with any of this. I know why you're here – and that self-pitying speech doesn't fool me. |
| **Paudge:** | No, nobody could ever fool you – but this minute, I could smash your little face back into that pig-tail of yours. |
| **Nick:** | And that'd get Jackie back, would it? |
| **Paudge:** | It might – but I mightn't need to do that tonight ... |
| **Nick:** | Oh thanks. |
| **Harry:** | *(To Jimmy)* See anything? |
| **Paudge:** | ... because when Jackie sees these old films, she might begin to realise a few things. |
| **Jimmy:** | *(High and leaning precariously)* Something here. |
| **Nick:** | *(To Paudge)* Oh yes – like you and her together? |
| **Paudge:** | You're forgetting something smart-arse! |
| **Nick:** | No, you're forgetting that she'll suddenly remember what you looked like at school – The Abominable Bog-Man – and wonder why she ever bothered with you. *(To Jimmy)* Our names up there, Jimmy? |
| | *(Nick goes to where Harry stands, holding the tables. Paudge will follow)* |
| **Jimmy:** | *(High up)* Yeah ... yeah ... I see 'Crazy Horse' and ... |
| **Harry:** | That's me folks. |
| **Paudge:** | *(To Nick)* And you're forgetting Jackie might see more than her and me in that film. |
| **Harry:** | Jaysas lads, don't tell me you two are starting on about Jackie! |
| **Paudge:** | I'm not talking at all about Jackie. |
| **Nick:** | Then what the hell are you slobbering about? |
| **Paudge:** | Or maybe you've all forgotten Gregory. |
| | *(Harry jumps in his anxiety. The tables move)* |
| **Jimmy:** | *(Panic)* Harry, hold them! |
| **Harry:** | Jesus Christ, Paudge, now you cut that out! |
| **Nick:** | *(Laughs)* Who the hell is Gregory? |

**Jimmy:** *(Unsteady on top)* Hold the tables, Harry!

**Paudge:** *(To Nick)* Oh so you have forgotten him, have you?

*(Thunder rolls)*

**Nick:** Forgotten? What's there to forget?

**Harry:** Paudge, knock it off, I'm serious, we don't want any of that kind of stuff here tonight.

**Paudge:** You mightn't want it but these films could give it to you anyway.

**Nick:** Listen, I don't know what the hell you're talking about.

**Paudge:** Well when Jackie sees Gregory you will.

*(Nick suddenly grabs Paudge)*

**Nick:** You start any of that and I swear to Christ it won't be just you or your Tipperary farm we'll be laughing at.

*(Harry leaves the tables to grab Nick. The tables come crashing down, Jimmy, above, screams and holds onto, and dangles from, the top ledge of the window)*

**Harry:** Cut it out, Nick!

**Jimmy:** *(Above)* Jesus, help me!

**Paudge:** *(To Nick)* So now you remember, do you?! Do you remember saying 'It was all my fault' ...

**Nick:** One more word out of you ...

**Harry:** For Christ's sake, Nick. *(Lets go of Nick to try and rebuild the tables for Jimmy)* Hold on, Jimmy!

**Paudge:** *(Imitates)* 'Poor Gregory was all my fault.'

**Harry:** Jesus, Paudge!

**Nick:** *(Attacks Paudge)* I'll knock your teeth in if you even ...

**Paudge:** *(Effortlessly pushes him away)* Ah stop panicking, pig-tail – there's no film of Gregory, there never was. Your secret is safe tonight and every night ...

**Harry:** Jump Jimmy, onto the table.

**Paudge:** ... because if you use your little brain, Maurice wasn't even there that day.

**Nick:** *(More controlled)* There? Where's there? I don't know what the hell you're talking about.

**Harry:**     Jump for Christ's sake!
                *(Jimmy drops onto the table and rolls onto the ground, unhurt but furious)*

**Jimmy:**    Jesus Christ, what the hell happened – I was left hanging up there, I could have killed myself.

**Harry:**    These two shaggers arguing – are you all right?

**Jimmy:**    I could have killed myself, I could have killed myself!

**Harry:**    *(Furious)* Jesus, Jimmy, is there a parrot in your family?

**Paudge:**   It's all right, Jimmy, it's all over now. *(Laughs at Nick)* But look at the panic in that face – not like the smug photograph in that big glossy magazine now ...

**Nick:**     *The Farmer's Journal*, was it?

**Harry:**    Lads!

**Paudge:**   The Young Designer 'relaxing in his favourite room that mixes simplicity with nostalgia'. Look at him now.

**Nick:**     You never changed – you're still Chief Sitting Bull-Shit.

**Harry:**    *(Angrily)* Look, that's the end of it – all I want to hear now is that we've heard the last of this. Do I have your word on this, Nick? Paudge?

**Paudge:**   Well unless I mention it casually to Jackie ...

**Nick:**     *(Goes towards him)* You do an I'll ...

**Harry:**    For Jesus' sake, end it – forget Jackie, Jackie made up her own mind a long time ago – and, for Christ's sake, forget Gregory too.

**Jimmy:**    *(Anxious)* Gregory? What ... what's this about ...?

**Harry:**    It's about nothing.

**Paudge:**   Because Nick knows Gregory is not in the film.

**Jimmy:**    What film?

**Harry:**    He's not in any film.

**Paudge:**   Of course he's not – Nick knows Maurice wasn't even there that day.

**Nick:**     *(Turns away)* I know nothing about any of this ...

**Harry:**    None of us do because there's nothing to know.

| | |
|---|---|
| **Jimmy:** | Well I certainly don't because I wasn't there. |
| **Harry:** | Will you let it drop! |
| **Jimmy:** | If you remember, I wasn't always an Apache, not always. |
| **Harry:** | Who's asking you? |
| **Jimmy:** | I mean, even up there, there's only four names – my name's not there and that proves ... |
| **Harry:** | Will you shut-up, Jimmy! Jesus, lads, I have blood pressure – I'm in no condition for this – Paudge, we're not here tonight for any of that kind of talk so you forget it – in fact let's all forget it and get on with this shaggin' reunion ... Okay with you, Paudge? Nick? |
| **Paudge:** | Okay. |
| **Nick:** | I know nothing about it anyway. |
| **Harry:** | Then that's the end of it. *(Begins to move back the tables)* |
| **Jimmy:** | And what about Gre ... Gregory? |
| **Harry:** | Are you deaf? Gregory doesn't come into it! All right? |
| **Jimmy:** | Yeah, right, right. He doesn't come into it and I wasn't there anyway. |
| **Harry:** | Now let's get this furniture back in place before Maurice ... *(Hears Maurice coming)* Oh Christ! *(Maurice, Deirdre and Jackie come in, chatting)* |
| **Deirdre:** | And, Maurice, you wouldn't think of a nursing home for him? |
| **Maurice:** | Ah no – he'd want to die in his own home. |
| **Jackie:** | That's very important. |
| **Maurice:** | *(Sees the room. Furious)* Oh for God's sake, what happened here? |
| **Harry:** | *(Carrying a table)* It's okay, Maurice. |
| **Maurice:** | It's not okay – I had everything in place ... |
| **Harry:** | We're putting it back. |
| **Paudge:** | *(Carrying a table back)* Jimmy climbed up to see our names – up there, like Little Rabbit. |
| **Jimmy:** | Squirrel! |
| **Maurice:** | *(Angrily)* But I had everything organised to just |

|  |  |
|---|---|
| | come back and show the film. |
| **Harry:** | (*Holding a table. Explodes*) Maurice look at me, I'm putting it back – what do you want me to do: burst a blood vessel for you, get a brain haemorrhage, have blood pumping out of my ears? What?! |
| **Maurice:** | (*Calmed*) No. Fine, Harry, fine. And thank you. |
| **Jackie:** | (*To Nick*) Are you all right, darling? |
| **Nick:** | Couldn't be better. (*Kisses her*) |
| **Maurice:** | And are all our names up there, Jimmy? |
| **Jimmy:** | All there, Maurice – and the date – 1978. |
| **Maurice:** | Excellent. Now everybody, if you will all begin to take your places for the film. (*Switches on the projector light*) All functioning. |
| **Harry:** | Paudge, you sit away from Nick. |
| **Deirdre:** | Is your name up there, Jimmy? |
| **Jimmy:** | (*Sharply*) Yes. |
| **Deirdre:** | And is it up as Jimmy or as Little Squirrel? |
| **Jimmy:** | (*Shouts*) What the hell does it matter – you asked if it's there and I'm telling you, yes, it's there! All right? |
| **Deirdre:** | No need to bite the face off me! (*Sits*) And what film is this, Maurice? |
| **Jimmy:** | Questions, questions, always butting in. |
| **Maurice:** | Oh this will bring it all back, Deirdre. |
| **Harry:** | And are all the Apaches in it? (*Sits*) |
| **Maurice:** | There are indeed – and Jackie too. |
| **Jackie:** | Oh God – I remember that cine camera, Maurice – you were always where no one suspected. |
| **Maurice:** | It is all to be enjoyed, Jackie – get us all into the mood of the old days here. |
| **Paudge:** | Watch out for Jackie and me, everybody. |
| **Harry:** | Paudge! |
| **Deirdre:** | I'm really looking forward to this. |
| | (*Maurice turns off the lights. The film begins to roll. First, hair lines squiggle across the wall. There is an ominous rumble of thunder*) |
| **Harry:** | (*Merrily, of the thunder*) Jaysas, I thought it was |

silent – that sounds like stereo, Maurice ...

**Maurice:** Very good, Harry – now everybody, watch out for the numbers – we want a good, loud countdown.

**Nick:** *(Quietly, of Paudge)* If some people *can* count!

**Harry:** Shut-up, Nick.

*(Now the numbers appear, beginning at ten, nine ...)*

**Maurice:** Come on – ten ... nine ...

**All:** *(Loudly joining in)* ... nine ... eight ... seven ... six ... five ... four ... three ... two ... one ... ZERO!

*Throughout all of this, the curtain has begun to slowly fall. It is fully down at 'two', as they wait for the film to begin)*

### END OF ACT ONE

# ACT TWO
# SCENE ONE

*Some minutes later. At rise of curtain, the film which began at the end of Act one, is being shown. All are sitting, drinking, watching it, enjoying it. The mood is very lively. Outside, the storm continues.*

*Projected onto the back wall (in a very amateur, silent film), we see a group of 16 year olds, on a day out in Powerscourt. They are a young Jimmy (thin), Paudge (big and strong), Harry (Fat), Nick (good-looking), Jackie (in a fashionable straw hat). Much posing for the camera. The film action is as indicated in the dialogue. All with much laughter and banter.*

*(Note: See appendix for suggested video shooting-script)*

| | |
|---|---|
| **Maurice:** | That is the end of Dalkey Island. This is the last bit – Powerscourt. |
| **Harry:** | Powerscourt? I was never in Powerscourt. |
| **Jimmy:** | We were all in Powerscourt. |
| **Harry:** | I was never in Powerscourt. |
| **Deirdre:** | Were you there, Jimmy? |
| **Jimmy:** | Course I was ...<br>*(A shot of the young Jimmy, Harry, Nick, Paudge and Jackie, facing the camera)*<br>... Look there's me! There's me, Deirdre. |
| **Deirdre:** | Oh yeah. |
| **Nick:** | And me! |
| **Harry:** | Where's me? |
| **Nick:** | Who's that, fatso? |
| **Harry:** | I'm there – handsome bastard. |
| **Jackie:** | Oh my God! |
| **Deirdre:** | Is that you, Jackie? |
| **Paudge:** | That's Jackie – with me. See us, Jackie? |
| **Jackie:** | Yes Paudge, I see us. |
| **Deirdre:** | What were you all doing in Powerscourt? |
| **Jimmy:** | Mitching. Look, we were the best of friends. |

*(A sequence of all at the stream)*

**Harry:** There's me again – organising everything.

**Nick:** I didn't know you were pregnant, Harry.

**Harry:** That's all muscle, pal. *(Of Nick)* Jaysas look – Robert Redford gone wrong.

**Nick:** Jealousy, Harry.

**Paudge:** And me and Jackie again.

**Harry:** You oul ram.

**Jackie:** Your bad mind, Harry.

**Nick:** And there's the straw hat! Maurice, that's how you remembered it!

**Maurice:** No, I haven't seen this film for years.

**Harry:** Ya bleedin' chancer.

*(A sequence of Jimmy with the hedgehog)*

**Deirdre:** *(Laughs)* Is that you, Jimmy?

**Harry:** That's him – the lonely man.

**Nick:** My God – were you on hunger-strike, Jimmy?

**Jimmy:** I was very fit, Nick.

**Deirdre:** What are you holding?

**Harry:** It's his sandwiches.

**Jimmy:** No, I remember – that was a dead hedgehog I found.

**Nick:** Good God.

**Jimmy:** You see – I was interested in pest control even then.

**Harry:** He has that hedgehog mounted over the fireplace to this very day.

*(Sequence of them swinging over the stream)*

**Harry:** Look, there's me – Tarzan.

**Nick:** That's not Tarzan – that's his monkey.

**Harry:** Shag off.

**Jimmy:** Oh wait, I remember this – this is good.

**Deirdre:** What happened?

**Paudge:** Oh yes – look at Robert Redford now – showing off his Mickey Mouse muscles.

**Nick:** I don't remember this.

**Maurice:** The camera never lies.

**Deirdre:** Why, what happened?

| | |
|---|---|
| **Jimmy:** | Just watch it, Deirdre – this was great. |
| **Harry:** | Nick thought he could do everything. |
| **Deirdre:** | And what happened, Harry? |
| **Jimmy:** | Will you wait, Deirdre – it's coming up. |
| | *(A cheer as Nick falls in)* |
| **Paudge:** | Look at Robert Redford now. |
| **Jackie:** | Nick, you fell in. |
| **Nick:** | I don't remember that. |
| **Harry:** | I do – Powerscourt was contaminated for years. |
| **Paudge:** | Robert Redford drenched. |
| **Harry:** | ... wearing the wet-look by Style-Line. |
| | *(The camera creeps up on Paudge kissing Jackie)* |
| **Deirdre:** | What's this now? |
| **Jimmy:** | Just watch the film, Deirdre. |
| **Harry:** | Ah Jaysas – feeding time in the zoo again. |
| **Paudge:** | I remember that day. |
| **Jackie:** | Was nothing sacred, Maurice? |
| **Maurice:** | I used to just point the camera, Jackie. |
| | *(A sudden sequence of everyone running from camera)* |
| **Paudge:** | What's this? |
| **Maurice:** | Oh yes – someone threw a stone at a parked car ... |
| **Harry:** | Yes, that was me. |
| **Jimmy:** | Yes and we all ran for our lives from the owner ... |
| **Harry:** | There's me running ... |
| **Paudge:** | Wobbling. |
| **Nick:** | We all got away ... |
| **Harry:** | Except Maurice who stopped to film us running ... |
| **Nick:** | And the owner of the car caught him and beat the shit out of him. |
| **Maurice:** | *(Enjoying this)* Not true, gentlemen, not true. |
| | *(A shot of Jimmy, Harry and Nick doing the established Apache dance. Jackie and Paudge sit watching them)* |
| **All:** | Look, it's our dance. |
| **Jimmy:** | Look at me, Deirdre. |
| **Deirdre:** | Jimmy, you're doing it. |
| **Jimmy:** | Course I was. |
| **Harry:** | *(Sings)* 'On the banks of the river ...' |

*(As Nick and Jimmy join in)*

**Maurice:** *(Sternly)* No gentlemen, no singing – singing is number five on the programme. *(They stop)* This is just for watching the film and commenting – no singing.

**Paudge:** Look at you and me, Jackie – look.
*(The dance ends. A group shot)*

**Jimmy:** Look at that – the best of mates. Apaches for life.
*(The film suddenly ends to a chorus of 'Ahhhh')*

**Maurice:** That's it, gentlemen – and lights please, Harry.

**Harry:** Let there be light – and you could see for miles!
*(Harry turns the lights on. Maurice begins to rewind the film)*

**Jackie:** God, but we were young.

**Jimmy:** Great memories, lads, great memories. *(To Deirdre)* See? – real mates.

**Harry:** I enjoyed that.

**Nick:** Told you you would – it was brilliant.

**Jackie:** Do you have any more film, Maurice?

**Maurice:** A whole suitcase of them.

**Jimmy:** Stick another one on so.

**Harry:** Yeah, away we go again, Maurice.

**Maurice:** *(Rewinding)* No, no, I'm afraid not: we have to keep order.

**Harry:** Just line another one up there. *(To all)* Everyone all right for gargle?

**Paudge:** Do you remember those days, Jackie?

**Jackie:** Of course I do, Paudge.

**Paudge:** And Nick, do you?

**Nick:** Sure – but all's well that ends well. What's next on the programme, Maurice?

**Harry:** More films and more drinking. *(Opens bottles)*

**Deirdre:** *(To all)* Did you all go anywhere else together?

**Nick:** We went everywhere: Bray, Dublin Mountains ...

**Jimmy:** ... The Hell-Fire Club, remember Howth Head, the Stillorgan Bowling Alley ...

**Harry:** We travelled the shaggin' world together – I even had my passport stamped in Malahide once.

| | |
|---|---|
| **Nick:** | We had to get visas for Malahide! |
| **Jimmy:** | *(To Deirdre)* See? Best of mates. |
| **Harry:** | And always singing our Apache song – let's hear it again, lads. *(Pounds the beat)* |
| | *(Nick, Harry, Jimmy and Paudge get into position and now sing and stomp the Apache dance)* |
| **Paudge/Nick/Jimmy/Harry:** | 'On the banks of the river, stood Running Bear, young Indian brave ...' |
| **Maurice:** | *(Loudly)* No, no, no, gentlemen, please ... |
| | *(They continue, with great enthusiasm ...)* |
| **Maurice:** | *(Eventually. Loud and furious)* Stoooop! |
| | *(They stop)* |
| **Harry:** | *(Angrily)* Jaysas, are we ever going to get to sing this song? |
| **Maurice:** | Yes Harry – but look at the blackboard – it's not next on the programme. |
| **Harry:** | Right, well then another film to keep the ball rolling. |
| **Maurice:** | The blackboard, Harry – next is the Apache reaction to the film. |
| **Harry:** | And what the hell's that? |
| **Maurice:** | We gather around the camp-fire and have a pow-wow about the old days as we remember them from seeing the film ... one at a time. |
| **Harry:** | Jesus Christ – and then we kneel down and say the rosary, do we? |
| **Nick:** | Let's just do it, Harry – then it's the sing-song after that. |
| **Jimmy:** | I want to play the drums on it. *(Beats the desk)* |
| **Harry:** | I'm the drummer – I was always the shaggin' drummer! |
| **Maurice:** | Gentlemen, the reactions now ... please! |
| | *(They sit in position – around the projector ...)* |
| **Jackie:** | Maurice, as Deirdre and I didn't get a chance at the retrospectives, I think the ladies should begin on the reaction to the film. |
| **Harry:** | How can you, you're not Apaches. |
| **Jimmy:** | And anyway, Jackie, Deirdre never gets up and |

|           | talks. |
|-----------|--------|
| **Deirdre:** | Yes I do. |
| **Jimmy:** | Deirdre, you don't. |
| **Deirdre:** | I don't in Sallynoggin because I never get the chance. |
| **Jimmy:** | (*Quieter*) And I think you've had enough to drink. |
| **Jackie:** | No Jimmy, she has wonderful stories ... |
| **Jimmy:** | I think I know better, Jackie. |
| **Deirdre:** | (*Petulantly*) Well then, I just want to correct something that was said earlier about me not wanting to be a nurse. |
| **Jimmy:** | (*Harder*) Don't start that, Deirdre. |
| **Maurice:** | Deirdre, this section has to apply to the film – it cannot be about anything else. |
| **Deirdre:** | It does apply to the film. |
| **Jimmy:** | How could it? |
| **Deirdre:** | Because in that film, you said you always wanted to be a pest controller ... |
| **Nick:** | That's right – the dead hedgehog. |
| **Jimmy:** | And what has that got to do ... ? |
| **Deirdre:** | The same as when I was at school, I always said I wanted to be a nurse. |
| **Jackie:** | Yes that's right – Cecily always said that. |
| **Jimmy:** | All her family said it, Jackie, and she became a nurse ... |
| **Deirdre:** | Yes, but I had to give it up when ... |
| **Jimmy:** | Deirdre, you didn't! |
| **Deirdre:** | (*Annoyed*) Your mother said to my mother in *our* house, in front of you and me, that a career and motherhood don't mix. |
| **Harry:** | It's a good point, Deirdre. |
| **Deirdre:** | It's not a good point, Harry. |
| **Jimmy:** | Deirdre! |
| **Deirdre:** | Because my mother didn't agree and I didn't agree and my sister Cecily didn't agree ... |
| **Jimmy:** | (*Annoyed*) Well don't blame me – I said nothing. |
| **Deirdre:** | (*Annoyed*) Exactly – you said nothing ... |
| **Jimmy:** | Because you could have stayed a nurse ... |

**Deirdre:** No, I could not!

**Jimmy:** Of course you could. *(To all)* I didn't care if she ...

**Deirdre:** Jimmy, you hated me being a nurse.

**Jimmy:** I did not – and I don't think we should ...

**Maurice:** *(Annoyed)* Is this about the film?

**Deirdre:** Jimmy, you did hate it!

**Jimmy:** Okay but only because you wanted children ...

**Deirdre:** No – *you* wanted children ...

**Jimmy:** ... and all I said was that you out nursing all night was no way to raise children.

**Deirdre:** *(Angrily)* Oh yes – but that didn't stop you telling me to hold onto my nurses uniform and to keep it smart and well-pressed ...

**Jimmy:** *(Angrily)* What the hell has that got ... ?

**Deirdre:** ... and then getting me to put it on for you whenever it suited you ...

**Jimmy:** For Christ's sake, Deirdre!

**Deirdre:** Well let me tell you the next time I put it on I'll be going back to nursing and not strutting around the bedroom calling myself your little Florence Nightingale!
*(Silence)*

**Harry:** *(Quietly)* Jays!

**Maurice:** *(Then. Awkwardly)* I think I may be correct in saying that none of this has anything to do with the film.

**Jimmy:** *(Quietly furious to Deirdre)* And this is what you've been telling Jackie, is it?

**Deirdre:** *(Repentant and quiet)* No it isn't – you dragged that out of me.

**Jackie:** *(Weakly)* She was just telling me about the wedding breakfast ...

**Harry:** *(Curious)* And, may I just say, that what you've been saying is no problem anyway – to be honest, the only reason I fancy air-hostesses is purely because of their uniform.

**Nick:** Sure, it's quite common.

**Harry:** *(Lightly)* Pal of mine used to fancy the ban gardaí.

And that worked out great for him – because now he's in jail.

**Jimmy:** (*Controlled*) I would just like to say that I have resisted making counter allegations here ...

**Deirdre:** I know, Jimmy, and I'm sorry if I ...

**Jimmy:** ... *and* that what was said is totally untrue.

**Deirdre:** All right Jimmy – but your mother did tell my mother ...

**Jimmy:** And I think we have all heard enough of it now.

**Deirdre:** I was only ...

**Jimmy:** And it has nothing – nothing! – whatsoever to do with our film or with the Apaches.

**Maurice:** Well yes, I did think that – but it does allow us to make the important point that the little confrontations we experience in life need never interfere with the basic affection we hold for each other. For example, my father can be extremely demanding of me ...

**Jimmy:** (*Angrily*) I am never demanding, never!

**Deirdre:** I didn't say you're ...

**Jimmy:** (*To Deirdre*) And it's never anything you don't want to do – in fact it's more often exactly what you *do* want to do ... which is why we are now living in Rathfarnham where I know nobody and where you can do what you bloody-well like!
(*Awkward pause*)

**Maurice:** (*Then*) Well, what I meant by demanding, in my father, is often his demand that I acknowledge that my late mother, God rest her, is still alive and that often, when he is not playing the piano for her, he will demand that a place be set for her at the dinner table and, when she doesn't arrive in for dinner, that I go out and find her.

**Harry:** And do you?

**Maurice:** Find her? She's dead, Harry.

**Harry:** No – go out.

**Maurice:** No – I just look around the house ... and then I usually say she must be gone out to play bingo and sometimes when I say that, he will suddenly ask me how can she go out to play bingo if she's already dead and buried.

**Harry:**      A good point.

**Maurice:**   And then he'll accuse me of trying to confuse him by pretending I'm looking for her – and then I usually shout at him and he begins to cry again and that's when I show him his insurance policies and tell him to face the situation and that there is no need to worry about death or dying or funeral arrangements or anything, because it comes to us all.

**Harry:**      *(Then)* Great. Well, before it comes to all of us, what's next on that programme there?

**Nick:**       *(Careful of the mood)* I think we're still on the Reactions.

**Harry:**      Oh right. *(Drinks)*

**Maurice:**   And unless I have grossly misunderstood Deirdre, the point she set out to make is that, although she didn't attain her ambition in remaining a nurse, she and Jimmy are still caring for each other in the same way that, despite his demands, I am still caring for my father and he depending on me.

**Deirdre:**   Well yes.

**Harry:**      Okay, now I think we can move on to the sing-song or another film or ...?

**Maurice:**   *(Sternly)* A moment, Harry. *(To Deirdre)* And that, I take it, brings us to the end of your reminiscence, Deirdre.

**Deirdre:**   Yes.

**Jimmy:**     Good.

**Maurice:**   And Jackie?

**Jackie:**     Oh I have none, none at all.

**Harry:**      I thought you had a stack, the way you were going on.

**Jackie:**     I just wanted Deirdre to tell the story of her wedding breakfast.

**Harry:**    But that would have nothing to do with the film so it wouldn't have qualified.

**Deirdre:**  No – but you have stories, Jackie, I mean stories that *are* about the film – like how you once went out with Paudge and now you're happily married to Nick and Paudge has a 200-acre farm ... where's it, Paudge?

**Paudge:**   In Tipperary.

**Deirdre:**  In Tipperary. Like, did everyone know about that because I didn't?

**Jimmy:**    How could you!?

**Maurice:**  It came as a surprise to me – but I think it should please all the Apaches gathered here that Paudge is happy and that it has worked out so well for Jackie and Nick and their little girl.

**Deirdre:**  Aoife.

**Jackie:**   Emma.

**Deirdre:**  Emma.

**Maurice:**  It's all like it was meant to happen – what was it the existentialist writer Camus once said: 'Where life assumes the aspect of destiny'.

              (*A small cheer*)

**Harry:**    Be Jaysas, that's raised the level of the evening.

**Jimmy:**    That's very good, Maurice.

**Deirdre:**  I can see now that you were the brain of the class, Maurice.

**Harry:**    We'd never have got an exam without him.

**Maurice:**  I think I read that quotation on a calendar.

**Jackie:**   Now now, humility will get you nowhere.

**Paudge:**   Do you want to correct anything about what was said there, Nick?

**Nick:**     No – I think that was a correct quotation.

**Paudge:**   About Emma.

**Nick:**     No.

**Paudge:**   Will I do it for you?

**Jackie:**   Paudge ... ?

**Harry:**    (*Anxiously*) Right, fine – now can we move onto something else ...

| Paudge: | No no, it has been mentioned – and I'm glad it has been mentioned because maybe some of you would like to know a bit more about Emma. |
| Maurice: | Well why not. |
| Nick: | *(Angrily to Paudge)* This is what you're here for isn't it? |
| Paudge: | I'm here for the reunion, Nick. |
| Nick: | After saying you wouldn't be coming. |
| Paudge: | If I said I was coming would Jackie be here? Damn sure she wouldn't, because you'd be afraid of a few home truths. |
| Jackie: | Paudge, stop it! |
| Paudge: | He didn't even want to see the film because ... |
| Jackie: | Well now he's seen it, we've all seen it, Paudge – seen you and me and me and you – now what the hell else do you want? |
| Paudge: | I want us to set the record straight. |
| Harry: | Now listen, this is exactly what we're not getting into here and I've already warned the two of you ... |
| Paudge: | I just want him to stop all this pretending and to say that Emma ... |
| Jackie: | Shut-up Paudge! |
| Paudge: | ... is not his child – it's not 'Nick, Jackie and Emma' because Emma is my little girl, born to me not to him ... |
| Nick: | Yes when you didn't want to know a damn thing about her or about Jackie. |
| Jackie: | Nick! |
| Paudge: | I wasn't let because you took Jackie ... |
| Nick: | Jackie ran! |
| Paudge: | And weren't you glad she ran to you to take you out of that poky little flat and fix you up in her shops. |
| Nick: | At least she wasn't stuck on a shitty farm. |
| Jackie: | Stop it! |
| Paudge: | She wouldn't have been stuck – and I'd've seen she had a *real* life ... |

**Nick:**     Oh yes, with your cave-man tactics ...

**Paudge:**   ... and not what she has to settle for from a
              window-dresser that spends his time putting little
              dresses on women dummies!

**Jackie:**   Will you shut-up, both of you!

**Deirdre:**  I'm sorry, I didn't mean to bring up about ...

**Jackie:**   It's all right, Deirdre, I knew this would happen.
              *(To Paudge)* We had all this once before when you
              came up to see Emma – I said then I never wanted
              it to happen again so I don't want another word
              about this out of either of you and that is final!
              *(Harry's phone rings)*

**Harry:**    Well said, Jackie – for the first time in my life I
              agree with you – like you, I can't shaggin' see
              why we can't have a civilised piss-up here with-
              out all this scrapping and fighting and I intend to
              sort it all out, once and for all – but now, a bit of
              quiet if you don't mind. *(Very affected into the
              phone)* Hello, Sun-Kissed Holidays, can I help
              you?

**Maurice:**  Harry, that might be my father because ...

**Harry:**    *(Into the phone delighted)* Paul, that is terrific, great.
              *(Listens)*

**Maurice:**  *(To all)* This is why I wanted the reunion in my
              house: when I go out, I always have this worry.

**Deirdre:**  But wouldn't the noise have kept him awake?

**Maurice:**  No no, he sleeps like a baby in the noise – it is the
              silence that keeps him awake.

**Harry:**    *(Into the phone)* You've made me a happy man,
              Paul – you have my permission to fondle Fiona
              first thing in the morning, right after me! *(Big
              laugh)* I like it – terrific. Right – keep in touch.
              Ciao. *(Clicks off. To all)* Great news: airport strike is
              over – happy days are here again.

**Nick:**     *(Sourly)* Good.

**Harry:**    *(Sees the mood)* Right. And now – Nick, Paudge,
              Jackie – I think I have a bit patching-up to do
              here.

**Jackie:**  This is not something that you just patch-up!

**Harry:**  Sorry Jackie, but I think it is and I'll give you two reasons why: One, in my business, I do a lot of patching up: missed connections, lost possessions, strikes, you name it I do it. And Two: this is an Apache reunion and the conflict here is between two Apaches and all our lives we've sorted out each others' conflicts.

**Maurice:**  And that's why we're here tonight – to face all our conflicts, past and present.

**Harry:**  Actually, Maurice, we're here for a piss-up! But, before we push on, let me attend to Nick and Paudge and Jackie.

**Jackie:**  (*Stands up*) Excuse me.

**Nick:**  Jackie, where are you going?

**Jackie:**  Not far and not for long – but out of here before I scream. (*Goes*)

**Maurice:**  Jackie ... ?

**Deirdre:**  Nick, do you want me to go with her ... ?

**Nick:**  No no – she often does this: she likes to get away on her own every now and then.

**Harry:**  Right, that's something else I understand in my business and in my life: the need to be alone – maybe another reason why I don't need a wife looking at me every time I walk into the kitchen.

**Deirdre:**  Harry, wives don't spend their time in the kitchen.

**Maurice:**  It's something, frankly, I would not be adverse to: a wife.

**Jimmy:**  One man's meat, I say.

**Harry:**  And there goes our parrot again – little joke, Jimmy – no offence. Now, here tonight, – and I feel somewhat responsible for this, it being here in the school at my suggestion – we've had a great film show and then a few upsets.

**Deirdre:**  And they were all my fault ...

**Harry:**  Well let's not place blame ...

**Deirdre:**  No, it was I who mentioned Emma and it was I

who attacked Jimmy in public ...

**Jimmy:** Just leave it now, Deirdre ...

**Deirdre:** *(Quiet and repentant)* No, Jimmy, I have to patch this up: I said you were demanding and I have to say now that that is not true ...

**Jimmy:** *(Quietly)* Deirdre, there's no need ...

**Deirdre:** There is, Jimmy, because I was wrong – and what I said we do is as much my choice as it is yours ...

**Harry:** *(Curious)* You mean the Florence Nightingale thing?

**Deirdre:** Well whatever I said ...

**Jimmy:** Jesus Christ, Deirdre!

**Deirdre:** No Jimmy, in fairness I also ask you to do things ...

**Jimmy:** There's no need to shout it all over the place!

**Deirdre:** I'm not.

**Harry:** *(Curious)* Jimmy, if Deirdre wants to patch it up ... *(Settles in to listen to Deirdre)* we should let her.

**Jimmy:** *(To Deirdre)* And will you for God's sake stop drinking that stuff!

**Deirdre:** All right – but I want to say that if I ever ask you to do anything, you do it – and you never throw it back in my face ...

**Jimmy:** Then leave it at that.

**Deirdre:** Even something stupid like the Fire Brigade Man ...

**Jimmy:** Oh Christ!

**Deirdre:** ... and you were right saying I got my way in moving to Rathfarnham and, even if I was right in saying you never wanted me to be a nurse, you were right in saying I wanted children but I didn't want them as rapidly as you did and I didn't want my whole life to be just cleaning the house and washing clothes and making meringues ... but I'm not unhappy, Jimmy – that's all I wanted to put right – all right?

**Jimmy:** Grand – now can we get onto something else?

**Deirdre:** *(To all)* I just had to say it because I think I've caused so much trouble here ...

**Harry:** But, Deirdre, all crises can be patched-up, just like my strike in Spain, just like what you've just done here ...

**Maurice:** I solve a lot of crises within myself and with my father by just getting him to talk it out ...

**Deirdre:** But I never had any idea about Emma when I mentioned her ...

**Maurice:** Well neither had I ...

**Harry:** Course you hadn't, none of us had – well I had – but listen, analyse it and you'll say 'what the hell's it all about?' Paudge here once went out with Jackie, they had a bambino – no sweat there: my own brother, an even bigger ram than myself, had three kids by two women and nobody even mentions it. So Paudge goes his way, to his big ranchero in Tipperary, in comes Nick and it's working out great.

**Maurice:** Very true.

**Harry:** Now, getting to Jacinta – or Jackie, as she calls herself now because she's into big fashion and I'm not criticising her for that – though never could I say, with my hand on my heart, that she's my favourite woman of all time – and why? Well maybe I don't like women muscling in among the lads, maybe I think she broke up the Apaches – but, that said, she came here tonight to enjoy herself and I don't think she deserves to be upset like that.

**Maurice:** Agreed, Harry.

**Deirdre:** Yes, that's not right.

**Harry:** So let's welcome her back, when she comes – patch all this up and have ourselves a helluva good reunion from now on.

**Maurice:** Absolutely – as per the programme.

**Harry:** *(Sharply)* As per shaggin' anything that keeps the party going and lets us enjoy ourselves!

**Deirdre:** Exactly. Everything all right now, Jimmy?

**Jimmy:**     Yes!

**Harry:**     Terrific – *(Curiously)* and, interestingly Deirdre, I was saying earlier how I fancied the air-hostesses because of their uniforms and you mentioned there something about the Fire Brigade Man.

**Deirdre:**   Ah that was nothing.

**Harry:**     No – just that a pal of mine once told me he was into that and he used to put on a fireman's helmet for his wife ...

**Deirdre:**   I'm afraid we don't have the helmet – we just have the boots ...

**Jimmy:**     Deirdre!

**Deirdre:**   No Jimmy, it's something *I* ask you to do, not you ask ...

**Harry:**     Sure, exactly – and, without interfering, what is it? – you just like Jimmy to be the fireman with the boots and to rescue you ...?

**Deirdre:**   Ah, no, no ...

**Jimmy:**     Why are we ... ?!

**Deirdre:**   ... it's Jimmy that lets me be the fireman and I break in and rescue him from the burning house – but it's all only a bit of fun.

**Harry:**     Oh. *(Considers this. Suddenly recovers)* Right. That's great. Okay – Nick, Paudge – all okay with you, before Jackie gets back?
               *(A flash of lightning across the shutters)*

**Nick:**      *(Quiet and hard)* I'd just like to make it clear that I am not a window-dresser.

**Harry:**     Point taken, Nick.

**Paudge:**    Except that I saw him doing it.

**Nick:**      I'm not saying I haven't done it ...

**Paudge:**    You were putting dresses on naked women dummies.

**Nick:**      I may well have been ...

**Paudge:**    You bloody-well were.

**Nick:**      ... and that is exactly what any top designer, with his own label, might be doing ...

**Paudge:**    Oh, a real man's job.

**Nick:**      *(Angrily)* Yes it is a real man's job – and if you have a problem accepting fashion design as a legitimate male profession, then you still are what you always were, a moron!

**Harry:**     Lads, lads ...

**Nick:**      And another thing – I never lived in a poky flat, here or in London ...

**Paudge:**    You never had a job in your life until Jackie took you in.

**Nick:**      And what were you before you were handed the farm?

**Harry:**     Now, that's it – we've had enough of that – and I don't want another word about it – when Jackie walks in here, I want us to be ...

               *(Jackie comes in. Thunder rumbles. She looks uneasy)*

**Deirdre:**   Ah Jackie – are you all right?

**Jackie:**    Oh fine. *(Small laugh)* But I don't think I'll go out there again in a hurry.

**Nick:**      Why, what's wrong, darling?

**Jackie:**    No, nothing.

**Harry:**     You didn't turn on the lights, did you?

**Jackie:**    No – but in a flash of lightning, I could have sworn I saw someone, just standing, looking up at this room.

**Nick:**      Where was this?

**Jackie:**    At the far end of the corridor ...

**Harry:**     Not the cops, is it?

**Nick:**      I'll go and have a look.

**Jackie:**    No no darling, it's all right, it was just my imagination because when I went down ...

**Deirdre:**   You went down?

**Jackie:**    Just a bit and there was nothing – but for a moment it looked like a young boy.

**Harry:**     Well Jaysas, if he's coming to school now, he's a bit late – 'out to the line, ya bastard!'

**Nick:**      Much more likely this plonk you've been drinking. *(With the bottle)* More?

**Jackie:**    *(Brightly)* Yes – may as well see the whole class arriving next time.

**Deirdre:** This is my fault too – frightening you, telling you about this room.

*(Thunder rumbles)*

**Harry:** Yeah well, it's all part of the fun – talking of which, Maurice, is there anything else on your programme before we can come onto the sing-song.

**Maurice:** Well unless anyone has any further comment on our film reactions ...

**Harry:** Did you have something, Jackie?

**Jackie:** No, nothing at all.

**Deirdre:** Well all I'd say – because I forgot to mention it earlier – was that I never knew that Jimmy wanted to do pest control when he was so young and I want to say it was great in the film to see him thinking of it. That's all.

**Maurice:** Yes and Jackie in her straw hat – thinking of fashion ...

**Harry:** *(Lightly)* And me showing you around Powerscourt – thinking of travel.

**Maurice:** What was it C. S. Lewis said 'Gratitude looks to the past, but ambition looks ahead'.

*(A cheer)*

**Harry:** Proud of you, Maurice – you spoofer.

**Nick:** Give us a cog of that, Maurice.

**Jimmy:** This is like the old days now, lads.

**Deirdre:** And Jimmy, I suppose you didn't put a name on that hedgehog in the film?

**Harry:** Yeah – prick.

**Jimmy:** A name?

**Jackie:** Oh yes, that's a good story, Jimmy.

**Jimmy:** What is?

**Jackie:** How you personalise each pest that you set out to eradicate. I love the one about the nest of wasps that you called 'The Mormon Tabernacle Choir'.

**Jimmy:** Who was telling you this, Jackie?

**Jackie:** Deirdre told me.

**Deirdre:** I said, in your profession, you always put names on them.

**Jimmy:** Oh yes. *(In his element)* Well you see, Jackie, it's all got very sophisticated in pest control now – personalising the pest is now quite a common psychological device.

**Harry:** Like you called the wasps a choir because they were singing or what?

**Jimmy:** No, it's just to give the enemy an identification – like I was once tracking down a species of Orthopterous – to the layman – cockroaches and I called them a family of Stephen Roches.

**Nick:** That's good.

**Harry:** Or a magpie could be called Maggie Thatcher.

**Jimmy:** Exactly.

**Nick:** Or a beetle could be called Ringo.

**Jimmy:** Now you have it.

**Jackie:** This would make a great parlour game.

**Paudge:** What would I call the badger that we can't catch on the farm?

**Nick:** *(Coldly)* Lucky?

**Harry:** *(Quickly)* He'd call him Jimmy because Jimmy himself is as grey as a badger.
*(Laughter)*

**Jackie:** So did you have a name on that hedgehog ...

**Deirdre:** In the film ...

**Jimmy:** I think I might have called him Brother Holmes!

**Harry:** Because he was always getting stuck into us!
*(Laughter)*

**Maurice:** And Deirdre was telling us you once had a mouse and you called it Gregory.
*(Sudden quietness)*

**Jimmy:** Pardon me?

**Maurice:** That's what Deirdre said – you had a mouse called Gregory.

**Jimmy:** What mouse? I never had a mouse.

**Jackie:** It was the one you were trying to kill and you called it Gregory.

**Maurice:** You used to wake up shouting his name.

**Deirdre:** No, Maurice, that's not true ...

**Jimmy:** I'm bloody sure it's not true ...

**Deirdre:** You didn't wake up – I used to have to waken you up because you'd be kicking and rolling around in the bed ...

**Jimmy:** What the blazes are you talking about?

**Deirdre:** In your sleep – you'd be shouting 'Gregory Gregory' and when I asked you who Gregory was, you said it was a mouse.

**Jackie:** Do you not remember him, Jimmy?

**Jimmy:** No and I don't know what the hell you're talking about ...

**Deirdre:** It was just after we got married ...

**Jimmy:** I don't care when it was, I don't remember it!

**Jackie:** That's probably because it was all in your dream, but Deirdre remembers it because it used keep her awake.

**Jimmy:** What? Yes, well maybe – I only know I don't remember it.

**Harry:** (*Finally*) Okay, fine, so that's that. Now, everyone okay for gargle?

**Maurice:** Though there was a boy named Gregory here, in school – does anyone remember him?

**Nick:** No.

**Harry:** Eh – no.

**Jimmy:** Me neither.

**Paudge:** I think I remember him.

**Harry:** Paudge!

**Maurice:** He was about two classes behind us ...

**Harry:** Jaysas, that's a great memory you have – seeing as how there was four hundred boys in the school.

**Maurice:** Maybe I just remember him because he was the first to die.

**Jackie:** Who was?

**Maurice:** Gregory.

**Deirdre:** He's dead?

**Jackie:** Did he die here in the school?

| | |
|---|---|
| **Maurice:** | No no, he was still at school, in sixth year, but he was drowned. The funeral was in Dean's Grange. |
| **Harry:** | Jas, I can't stand funerals. |
| **Maurice:** | I remember the traffic was jammed up for hours ... |
| **Deirdre:** | Were you at it, Maurice? |
| **Maurice:** | I think we were all at it – the whole school, the staff, present and past pupils. I was in the seminary at the time: I have a memory of you laughing at my Roman collar, Harry. |
| **Harry:** | Me? Oh yeah, I think I remember a funeral all right ... |
| **Jimmy:** | That's right, there was a big funeral we were all at – the whole school, past pupils and all. |
| **Jackie:** | Were you there, Nick? |
| **Nick:** | Could have been – I tend to forget funerals. |
| **Deirdre:** | Were you, Paudge? |
| **Paudge:** | We were all there. |
| **Jimmy:** | That's right we all went because he was still at school: Gr ... Gregory. |
| **Harry:** | I remember that now – whether we knew him or not, we all went – past pupils, staff, everyone ... and, for us, it was a chance to meet all the Apaches again. |
| **Nick:** | It was the only time we all did meet. |
| **Deirdre:** | And was he out swimming or what – when he drowned? – Gregory. |
| **Harry:** | Yes, I ... |
| **Maurice:** | No, he was fully dressed. Some people thought, at first, that he had been murdered ... |
| **Jackie:** | Murdered? |
| **Maurice:** | I think that's the real reason so many were at the funeral ... |
| **Jackie:** | I don't remember this at all. |
| **Paudge:** | Oh I remember it clearly. |
| **Maurice:** | Though later they decided it was suicide. |
| **Harry:** | I never heard that, to be honest. |
| **Jimmy:** | Me neither. |

**Nick:**     Nor I.

**Harry:**     I assumed it was an accident – natural causes.

**Maurice:**     Ah no – they found witnesses, passers-by, who saw him down Dun Laoghaire pier, at the end, looking into the water, walking away, coming back again to look in ... and then they missed him. His body was recovered two days later.

**Jackie:**     Did you know him well, Maurice?

**Maurice:**     Not really – but afterwards, I kept in touch with his family – I used to go to see them occasionally – this was after I left the seminary: well I felt that if I could do something for them, get them to come to terms, try to live life positively – as I do selling my insurance policies. Although, professionally, I was of little help – suicide disqualifies most insurance claims.

**Jackie:**     Yes, of course.

**Deirdre:**     In nursing, we see death, but suicide is so upsetting.

**Maurice:**     And Gregory's diary was most upsetting – his parents showed that to me.

**Paudge:**     His diary?

**Maurice:**     Yes – most upsetting.
          (*Short pause*)

**Jimmy:**     Funny, now that I come to think of it, I think I do remember that mouse called Gregory, the one I couldn't catch, years ago.

**Jackie:**     The one in your nightmare?

**Jimmy:**     Yes, that just came back to me now.

**Deirdre:**     So I was right?

**Jimmy:**     I think you were, yes – there was a mouse I had a terrible time tracking down ...

**Deirdre:**     Oh yes, you used to wake up in an awful state, you'd be roaring out his name – (*Loudly*) 'Gregory, Gregory ...'

**Jimmy:**     All right!

**Deirdre:**     And you'd be all rigid and soaked in perspiration: (*Loudly*) 'Gregory, Gregory ...'!

**Jimmy:**    *(Louder)* There's no need to go on – I said I re-
              member it! *(Calmer)* But as for your Gregory,
              Maurice, I can remember the big funeral, but not
              him. Terrible, isn't it?

**Harry:**    Well, same as myself.

**Nick:**     Course it was a long time ago.

**Harry:**    Can't put a face on him at all.

**Jackie:**   But isn't that so sad.

**Harry:**    Oh desperate.

**Maurice:**  Well, gentlemen, I think I may be able to help you
              there.

**Harry:**    Sorry, Maurice?

**Maurice:**  I may be able to jog your memory of what Greg-
              ory looked like.

**Deirdre:**  Do you have a photograph, Maurice – I love old
              photographs.

**Maurice:**  Better than that. *(Goes to his suitcase)* I may have
              him on film.

**Nick:**     On film?

**Jackie:**   Oh great.

**Harry:**    What film is this, Maurice?

**Maurice:**  I have them all catalogued by date – I think it was
              the year we left school, sixth year.

**Deirdre:**  Aren't you great to keep them.

**Nick:**     But where would you be filming Gregory ... ?

**Paudge:**   *(To Nick)* Good question.

**Jackie:**   Maurice had his camera everywhere – you'd be
              doing anything and suddenly you'd hear this
              whirring noise, turn around and there he'd be.

**Harry:**    So what's the film of, Maurice?

**Maurice:**  *(Takes one out)* '1977. The woods'. This could be it.

**Jimmy:**    *(Anxiously)* The woods?

**Nick:**     Maurice, I don't think we need to see that film.

**Maurice:**  *(Looking)* It mightn't be it.

**Jimmy:**    *(To Harry, anxiously)* It couldn't be it.

**Paudge:**   I think we should see it anyway.

**Jackie:**   Of course we should.

**Harry:**    *(Authoritatively)* And I think we shouldn't and I'll give you two reasons why not: One, this is our reunion and we hardly want to spend it looking at a poor unfortunate kid who committed suicide. And two, there is a programme on that blackboard that we have all agreed to – and any deviation from it has been totally forbidden – so why should we deviate from it now? The film is not on the programme so, sorry, it is out.

**Deirdre:** But surely it'd be no harm to ...

**Jimmy:** Will you stop butting in ...

**Maurice:** It's only about three minutes, Harry.

**Harry:** Sorry Maurice, that's your programme and it's not on it.

**Maurice:** I still think we should – I found it most helpful ...

**Jackie:** Why don't we put it to a vote?

**Deirdre:** Yes, a vote.

**Jimmy:** You can't vote – you're not an Apache.

**Maurice:** I think we should all vote and all abide by that democratic decision – in the same way, Harry, as you said that breaking in here was democratic.

**Jackie:** Yes, that's fair.

**Harry:** Right! Fine! Okay! *(To Paudge and Nick)* You two remember what we agreed ... *(to all)* now who wants to see it?
*(Maurice shoots his hand up, then Jackie and then Deirdre)*

**Jimmy:** Deirdre!

**Deirdre:** *(Keeps her hand up)* No Jimmy!

**Maurice:** Come on Nick, Harry, Jimmy, Paudge – let's all see it.

**Harry:** Still two reasons, Maurice – one, not on the programme, two, you're out-voted. Sorry.

**Jackie:** Nick!

**Nick:** It's not on the programme, darling.
*(Paudge has raised his hand)*

**Deirdre:** *(Indicates Paudge's hand)* Harry?

**Harry:** Paudge – what the hell's that?

**Paudge:** It's my hand, Harry.

| | |
|---|---|
| **Maurice:** | Good man, Paudge. |
| **Nick:** | For God's sake! |
| **Harry:** | Paudge, you shaggin' promised! |
| **Paudge:** | In the interests of fair play, lads. |
| **Maurice:** | Four to three: excellent – I'll line it up. *(Goes to his projector with the film)* |
| **Nick:** | *(To Paudge)* You bastard – you're not getting away with this. |
| **Jackie:** | It's all right, Nick – it's only three minutes. |
| **Harry:** | *(Quietly to Nick)* And it couldn't be it. |
| **Jimmy:** | *(Angrily to Deirdre)* And this is your idea of patching it up with me? |
| **Deirdre:** | Jimmy, it'll be like the other one. |
| **Harry:** | *(Quietly to Nick)* We'll just watch it. |
| **Nick:** | Will we? *(Goes to the door)* |
| **Jackie:** | Nick, are you all right? |
| **Nick:** | Back in a minute. *(Goes angrily)* |
| **Paudge:** | *(Calls)* Don't worry, we won't start till you get back, Running Bear. |
| **Jackie:** | Be careful, Nick, it's very spooky out there. *(A low rumble of thunder as Deirdre and Jackie look through Maurice's film collection, as Maurice sets up the film)* |
| **Jimmy:** | *(Anxiously)* Harry, do you think ... ? |
| **Harry:** | *(Angrily)* Shut-up! *(Harry goes to Paudge. Jimmy follows)* |
| **Harry:** | Okay Paudge, what's going on here? – I thought you agreed not to mess up this night ... |
| **Paudge:** | Who's messing it up – let him show the film – he wasn't there when you ... |
| **Harry:** | He was shaggin' everywhere ... |
| **Paudge:** | Do you remember him being there? |
| **Harry:** | No – but that doesn't mean ... |
| **Jimmy:** | And what about his diary? |
| **Harry:** | Will you shut-up and stop panicking. *(To Paudge)* And I know why you're doing this – shaggin' women – they mess up everything. *(Harry will go to Maurice. Jimmy to Deirdre. Paudge* |

*to Jackie)*

**Jimmy:** Deirdre, if you want to go home, you can take the car ...

**Deirdre:** Why would I want to go home ...

**Jimmy:** Well you keep saying that this place is spooky and like a mausoleum and ...

**Deirdre:** No Jimmy, I'm grand.

**Jimmy:** *(Quietly and furiously)* Why can you never do what you're bloody-well told!

**Harry:** *(To Maurice)* Maurice, this film – what's it of, exactly.

**Maurice:** Very little, but Gregory is in it.

**Harry:** Am I in it?

**Maurice:** Harry, listen, after I left the seminary, I used to look at it all the time and I found it helped my dreams and it will help your dreams *(Quieter)* and poor Jimmy's too, God help him.

**Harry:** There's nothing the matter with my dreams – I just want to know now what exactly that film ...

**Maurice:** We all need to face it, Harry.

**Harry:** Face what? There's nothing to face!

**Maurice:** And do you know what the last entry in his diary was?

**Harry:** Diary? No, what was it?
*(Harry's phone rings)*

**Maurice:** Oh Harry – I think I should have phoned my father earlier in case he ...

**Harry:** *(Takes out his phone)* Now you listen here – if you show that film, you are phoning nobody – and I don't care if your father is roaring his head off or strangling himself or dancing naked on the top of his shaggin' piano. *(Affected, into the phone)* Hello, Sun-Kissed holidays – can I help you? Ah Paul.

**Paudge:** *(To Jackie)* Nice to see us both together again – in the voting.

**Jackie:** Is it?

**Paudge:** Jackie, you know I still want to see you and I think you secretly would like us to ...

**Jackie:** Paudge, would you ever wise up.

**Paudge:** And I have a right to see Emma so we could ...

**Harry:** *(Angrily into phone)* But you said we were clear!

**Jackie:** *(To Paudge)* Paudge, if you think you can use Emma in this, then you have a short memory – but I haven't. *(Moves away)*

**Harry:** *(Into phone)* Then let the shaggers sit there – it wasn't our fault – end of story. *(Clicks off)* Every charter flight is taking off, except us: this is because we're Irish.

**Jackie:** But I thought you were good at patching things up.

**Harry:** I'm in no mood for you, Jacinta *(To Maurice)* ... or that shaggin' film either.

**Deirdre:** Will I turn off the lights, Maurice?

**Maurice:** No, just running it to the beginning of the film.

**Jackie:** Ah Nick!

*(Nick comes into the room, closing the door. Behind his back, he carries a laboratory bottle of clear fluid)*

**Deirdre:** Nick, we're all waiting for you.

**Jimmy:** *(Anxiously)* The film is all ready and ...

**Nick:** Sorry for keeping you – I was looking around some old classrooms ...

**Maurice:** Nick, looking around old classrooms is not on our programme ...

**Harry:** And neither is this film.

**Nick:** ... including the old science room – and it's really amazing down there: everything's the very same: bunson burners, tripods, bottles, bits of phosphorus in jars ... things I was once very interested in ...

**Maurice:** Now wait a minute, Nick ...

**Nick:** And, looking around, I got this. *(The bottle)*

**Harry:** What's that, Nick?

**Nick:** This, it says here is *(Reads)* 'Dangerous ... sulphuric acid.'

**Jackie:** Now Nick, you've had too much to drink ...

**Nick:** And I am now proposing, as Running Bear of the Apaches, an addition to the programme – a new

Indian ritual.

**Paudge:** No, you are not!

**Maurice:** Nick, next on the programme is the sing-song ...

**Nick:** And for this ritual, I propose to borrow Deirdre's cake tin – you don't mind, do you, Deirdre ... ?

**Deirdre:** (*Anxiously*) Jackie?

**Jimmy:** No, she doesn't mind, Nick – go on.

**Maurice:** Nick ... ?

(*Nick has taken the cake tin and un-corked the laboratory bottle*)

**Nick:** And being very very careful ... (*Begins to pour the acid into the tin*)

**Jackie:** Nick, please – you're in no condition for that kind of carry-on.

**Nick:** (*As he does it*) Do any of you remember when Mr Conroy – Einstein Conroy – let a tiny drop splash onto his hand, the way he screamed when it burned through like a hot poker into wood? – Well we don't want that.

**Maurice:** Now Nick, as organiser of this reunion ...

(*Nick places the tin on a desk and stands back*)

**Nick:** Now, what I propose for this Indian ritual, is that we very carefully and ceremoniously take the film from the projector, carry it to this tin and there let it die painlessly in the acid so that it may go from us to the Happy Hunting Ground, where it belongs.

**Paudge:** Now you just wait a minute ...

**Jackie:** Nick you can't possibly be serious.

**Nick:** And as we believe in democracy, I suggest that the Apaches indicate their desire for this ceremony, by a show of hands. I say yes. (*Raises his hand*)

**Harry:** I say yes.

**Jimmy:** I say yes!

**Deirdre:** Jimmy, that's not your film!

**Nick:** That's a majority – three of the five Apaches.

**Jackie:** Well I say No.

| | |
|---|---|
| **Deirdre:** | And so do I. |
| **Paudge:** | I'm telling you all now, that nobody is touching that film. |
| **Harry:** | You're out-voted, Paudge – and you, ladies, are not Apaches. |
| **Jackie:** | We have a say – we had a say before. |
| **Harry:** | (*Angrily*) You've had a say in the Apaches for too shaggin' long – well you've no say here, Miss Big-Shot Jacinta! |
| **Nick:** | Knock it off, Harry. |
| **Maurice:** | Well I have a say ... |
| **Nick:** | It's a democratic decision, Maurice. |
| **Jackie:** | But why? Why destroy a film ... ? |
| **Paudge:** | I'll bloody-well tell you why ... |
| **Nick:** | You'll tell her nothing ... |
| **Maurice:** | Gentlemen, please ... |
| **Nick:** | So here's what we're doing, Maurice – Jimmy will go to the other room and disconnect the plug from the projector ... |
| **Deirdre:** | You will not, Jimmy. |
| **Harry:** | I'll do it. |
| **Paudge:** | Don't try it, Harry – we are showing that film. (*Harry stops*) |
| **Nick:** | ... and what we don't want is an accident with this acid ... |
| **Jackie:** | For God's sake, no one has the right to take Maurice's film ... |
| **Nick:** | Yes we have, Jackie – it's an Apache decision ... |
| **Jackie:** | (*Furious*) Christ, Nick, I'm surprised at you being so childishly stupid ... |
| **Paudge:** | You'd be more surprised, Jackie, if you saw the film ... |
| **Nick:** | Don't you start, Paudge ... |
| **Paudge:** | (*Angrily*) ... because, Jackie, what the great manly Nick doesn't want you to see in that film ... |
| **Harry:** | Paudge – shut-up! |
| **Paudge:** | (*Loudly*) ... is him dressing-up Gregory like one of your naked dummies in Wicklow Street ... |

**Harry:**  Oh for Christ's sake, lads!

**Nick:**  *(Furious)* That is not true!

**Paudge:**  It is true!

**Nick:**  *(Shouts)* And I did that on my own, did I?

**Paudge:**  Yes, you did!

**Nick:**  Then you're forgetting it was your idea to capture him, to get him to the woods, you were the one who held him when he struggled ...

**Paudge:**  Get it right – Harry held him!

**Harry:**  Me? I held no one!

**Nick:**  All right, Harry held him but then it was you who told Jimmy to cut the braces off his trousers ...

**Deirdre:**  *(To Jimmy)* What?

**Paudge:**  It was not – and all that was only messing for me, but you had the ...

**Nick:**  Okay – Jimmy who told you to cut Gregory's braces ... ?

**Jimmy:**  *(Panic)* What braces – I don't know anything about braces.

**Maurice:**  Admit it, Jimmy.

**Nick:**  *(To Jimmy)* The braces on Gregory's trousers – who told you to cut them?

**Paudge:**  *(To Nick)* You did!

**Nick:**  Wrong! You told him – you told Jimmy.

**Deirdre:**  *(Loudly to Jimmy)* What were you doing?

**Jimmy:**  I wasn't there!

**Paudge:**  *(To Nick)* And don't deny it was your idea to tie him to the tree ...

**Nick:**  I didn't do that!

**Maurice:**  *(Angrily)* Admit it!

**Harry:**  Jesus Christ, no one did any of this!

**Nick:**  It was Harry brought the rope.

**Harry:**  What rope?

**Paudge:**  *(To Nick)* Okay Harry brought the rope – but you had the dress and the lipstick ...

**Deirdre:**  My God!

**Nick:**  That was crayon, not lipstick.

**Paudge:**  You used it on Gregory as lipstick ...

Jimmy:      I wasn't there.
Paudge:     For Christ's sake, we were all there – the Apaches
            planned it ...
Jimmy:      No, not me – my name's not up there. *(The win-
            dow)*
Maurice:    Yes Jimmy, you were there, climbing the trees ...
Jimmy:      *(To Maurice)* How do you know – you weren't
            there!
Paudge:     You jumped down when Gregory started shout-
            ing ...
Jimmy*:*    *(To Paudge)* Because you ran away when he start-
            ed shouting ...
Deirdre:    *(To Jimmy)* So you were there!
Paudge:     I ran because I'd seen enough – *(To Nick)* – but
            you stayed there ...
Nick:       I did not stay ...
Harry:      No one stayed – Nick and I just left him to untie
            himself and go home ...
Jimmy:      And I was gone then ...
Nick:       *(Shouts to Paudge)* And I know why you're doing
            this ...
Paudge:     *(To Nick)* And at the funeral, you said ...
Harry:      Shut-up Paudge ...
Paudge:     Are you listening, Jackie – at the funeral in Dean's
            Grange he said 'This is all my fault'.
Nick:       I said 'Your fault' because you planned capturing
            him, in this very room, you said 'let's capture the
            little fairy ...'
Paudge:     At the funeral you said 'All my fault' ...
Harry:      It was nobody's fault because Gregory didn't
            mind it ...
Paudge:     Don't talk shite – he was crying ...
Harry:      It was only messing and Gregory knew that ...
Jimmy:      Yes, he was laughing when I left.
Paudge:     Laughing? – next you'll tell me he was laughing
            at his funeral.
Maurice:    The last entry in his diary was ...
Harry:      Will you shut-up!

**Maurice:** The last entry was 'I am not, I am not, I am not!'

**Nick:** What the hell does that mean?

**Harry:** It means nothing!

**Maurice:** You know what it means, Harry – you visit his grave ... Jimmy, you scream his name in your sleep ...

**Jimmy:** I do not!

**Maurice:** ... I left the seminary because of it ...

**Harry:** *(To Maurice)* Jesus Christ, you're twisting it all around ...

**Maurice:** We are all responsible so let's see the film – let's see him ... face up to it.
*(Maurice switches on the projector. Images, unclear in the light of the room, appear on the wall)*

**Nick:** We're seeing nothing.
*(Nick runs at the projector. He is held by Jackie)*

**Jackie:** No, Nick, no!

**Nick:** Get your hands off me. *(Struggles)*

**Harry:** I'll get the plug ...

**Paudge:** I warned you!
*(Harry has run towards the partition room, Paudge hits him. Harry goes down and lies still)*

**Jimmy:** I'll get the film, Nick.

**Maurice:** No ...
*(Jimmy runs at the projector. Maurice confronts him. They struggle. As they do, Deirdre runs to the projector and takes the film from it. The projector light goes out)*

**Maurice:** My film!

**Deirdre:** It's all right, Maurice – they won't get it.

**Jimmy:** Give that to me, Deirdre.

**Deirdre:** No, I want to see what you were up to.

**Jimmy:** I'm warning you, Deirdre. *(Runs at Deirdre)*

**Deirdre:** Jackie!
*(She throws the film to Jackie who catches it)*

**Nick:** Jackie, give me that film now. *(Moves towards her)*

**Jackie:** No Nick. Paudge? *(Holds it to throw to Paudge)*

**Nick:** For God's sake, Jackie.

| | |
|---|---|
| **Maurice:** | You must see it – you can't ignore it! |
| **Paudge:** | Throw it to me, Jackie. |
| **Nick:** | *(Calm and furious)* Jackie, that's the bastard who dumped you, who hit you, who didn't want to know you when you were pregnant ... |
| **Jackie:** | Nick, you have no right to destroy this film. |
| **Maurice:** | *(To Jackie)* They won't take the responsibility. |
| **Paudge:** | Come on, throw it, Jackie. |
| **Nick:** | *(Goes to her)* Jackie, I'm warning you, if you give that to him, it only means one thing to me. |
| **Paudge:** | Come on, Jackie. |
| | *(As Nick comes to her, Jackie throws it to Paudge)* |
| **Nick:** | *(Furiously)* Right, that's it, we're finished! |
| | *(Paudge clumsily drops the film. Harry, on the ground, grabs it)* |
| **Harry:** | Too late, Paudge. |
| **Paudge:** | Is that so? |
| | *(Paudge picks up Harry and throws him against the wall, grabbing the film from him. Paudge then turns to find himself now facing Nick, who has picked up the acid. All stop. From now to the end of the scene, the storm will gradually become more vicious: lightning will seem to angrily cross the window through rumbles and cracks of thunder)* |
| **Nick:** | *(Calmly)* Okay Paudge – hand it over. |
| **Jackie:** | *(Calmly)* Nick, put that down – that's dangerous. |
| **Nick:** | Shut-up you, I know who's side you're on ... |
| **Jackie:** | Nick, I'm not! |
| **Nick:** | ... and if he doesn't hand that over now, this acid goes right into his face. |
| **Deirdre:** | Oh my God. |
| **Harry:** | For Jesus' sake, Nick. |
| **Paudge:** | You wouldn't have the courage, Nick. |
| **Nick:** | Think, Paudge – because if you force me, not even your cattle will recognise you, never mind your precious little Emma. |
| **Maurice:** | Nick, we all have to face it, but let's ... |
| **Nick:** | *(Angrily)* He won't have a face if he doesn't hand |

that film over, now!

**Harry:** There's nothing on it, Nick – Maurice wasn't even there.

**Paudge:** He was there all right.

**Harry:** He shaggin' wasn't.

**Paudge:** He was – I passed him when I was running away, hiding with his camera ...

**Harry:** *(To Maurice)* What?

**Maurice:** I only went and untied him and filmed a tiny bit – but let's see that bit – Nick, it is only Gregory ...

**Nick:** Paudge, that film now or you get the acid into your face and your eyes ...

**Harry:** Ah Nick, no shaggin' film is worth this ...

**Maurice:** Nick, listen, I used to feel guilty too until I faced up to ...

**Nick:** Shut up! Paudge, I'll tell you exactly what I'm going to do ...

**Paudge:** And I'll tell you exactly what I'm going to do ...

**Maurice:** Can you all not just admit ...

**Nick:** I'm going to count to three ...

**Paudge:** And while you're doing that, I'm going to walk past you, out that door, with this film in my hand ...

**Nick:** No Paudge, you are not – and the count is 'one'.

**Jackie:** Oh Jesus, this is madness.

**Paudge:** And I'm going. *(Steps)* One. *(Stops)*

**Deirdre:** God, if he throws that acid ...

**Jimmy:** Shut-up!

**Harry:** He'll do it, Paudge – he's had a lot of booze taken ...

**Deirdre:** *(To Jimmy)* Do something!

**Paudge:** No he won't – he's only good for dressing up ladies dummies and young boys.

**Nick:** By Christ, you're asking for it – and the count is 'two'. *(Holds the tin towards Paudge)*

**Paudge:** And I'm on my way. *(Takes another step)*

**Harry:** For Jesus' sake, Paudge, will you stop moving! Listen, Nick ...

**Deirdre:** Jimmy! Do something!

**Jimmy:** Right! *(Opens the blade from his bottle-opener. Moves forward, almost hysterical with fear)* Okay Nick, freeze right there. Put down that acid – I'm behind you and I have a knife ...

**Nick:** Stay out of it, Jimmy ...

**Jimmy:** No – you put that acid down now ...

**Deirdre:** He has a knife, Nick.

**Jimmy:** And I'm not afraid – I'm trained to deal with wild rats and nests of wasps – I'm not afraid ...

**Paudge:** I'm going, Nick ...

**Nick:** I swear I will, Paudge. *(Holds the tray higher)*

**Jackie:** Nick!

**Maurice:** *(Furiously)* Wait, you bastards – why can't you take the blame ...

**Harry:** *(To Maurice)* You'll answer for this ...

**Paudge:** I'm going past you ...

**Nick:** I'll do it, Paudge!

*(A crack of thunder as Paudge tries to run past Nick. Jimmy runs at Nick with the knife. Nick throws the acid into Paudge's face. Paudge falls screaming, holding his face. The film falls to the ground. Seconds later, Jimmy has stabbed Nick in the shoulder. He cries out, but grabs the film to tear it to pieces. Jackie screams and runs to Paudge. Deirdre with her, but now taking control)*

**Jackie:** *(By his side)* Oh my God, Paudge!

**Deirdre:** *(In control)* Jackie, get back from him. Lie still, Paudge. Harry, phone for an ambulance.

**Harry:** What? Oh right. Nine nine nine. *(Takes out his mobile)*

**Nick:** *(Ripping the film)* I'll finish this once and for all ...

**Maurice:** Jesus Christ, this should never have happened.

**Paudge:** *(Writhing)* The eyes are burned out of me.

**Deirdre:** Take your hands down – let me see.

**Harry:** *(To Maurice, as he dials)* Now are you satisfied, you shaggin' lunatic?

**Maurice:** Why didn't you all just face up to it?

**Harry:**     To shaggin' what?

**Maurice:**   To what you all did – it wasn't just me but it was me he called the pervert.

**Harry:**     What? *(Into phone)* Hello! Hello!

**Jackie:**    *(Looking at Paudge)* Oh Christ, his face is destroy-ed.

**Deirdre:**   *(To Jackie)* Will you shut-up! Open your fingers, Paudge.

**Maurice:**   *(Loudly to Harry)* I was only untying him – why did he call me a pervert ... ?

**Harry:**     Stop shaggin' shouting at me. *(Of his mobile)* What's wrong with this! Hello!

**Maurice:**   Why should I be the only one to take the blame ...

**Nick:**      *(Realises)* Jesus, look, blood. *(To Jimmy)* You little bastard – you knifed me – look!

**Jimmy:**     You blinded Paudge – the eyes are burned out of him.

**Nick:**      They're not!

**Harry:**     *(Into his phone)* Ambulance service and quick.

**Jimmy:**     *(To Nick)* Look at him – look what you did with the acid.

**Nick:**      That's not acid – that's water.

**Harry:**     *(Into his mobile)* Emergency. Could we have an ambulance at once.

**Jimmy:**     Water? What's water?

**Jackie:**    Water?

**Deirdre:**   Yes – it's on my hands – it's only water ...

**Harry:**     *(To all)* Is it not acid?

**Nick:**      For Christ's sake, do you think they'd leave acid lying around – that's only water from the tap.

**Deirdre:**   Cancel the ambulance.

**Harry:**     *(Into his mobile)* Sorry, cancel the ambulance – it's only water from the tap. *(Clicks off)* What the hell is going on?

**Deirdre:**   Sit up, Paudge, that is only water.

**Nick:**      I only wanted to drop the film into water – but look at what that bastard has done to me – blood ... I'm bleeding to death.

*(Nick takes his hand from his arm. It is covered in blood)*

**Jackie:**    Oh my God, Deirdre – over here, quickly!

**Harry:**    Oh Jesus, Nick – that looks deep.

**Deirdre:**    *(To Harry)* Shut-up! *(Goes to Nick)* Stand back. Lie down, Nick. Harry, phone an ambulance.

**Harry:**    What? Oh right. Nine nine nine. *(Dials out)*

**Nick:**    *(To Deirdre)* Your stupid husband did this.

**Deirdre:**    Lie still, Nick. *(To Jimmy)* You and your knife.

**Jimmy:**    You told me!

**Deirdre:**    I suppose that's the same knife you cut Gregory's trousers off with. *(To all)* I want clean handkerchiefs. Tear something for a bandage.

**Jackie:**    Oh Nick, my darling ...

**Nick:**    *(Angrily)* Don't 'darling' me – you threw the film to Paudge, it's always been Paudge ...

**Jackie:**    Don't say that, Nick.

**Paudge:**    *(Blinking)* If that's only water, why can't I see?!

**Harry:**    *(Into his mobile)* Ambulance service – and quick.

**Deirdre:**    *(Looking)* We don't need an ambulance – the wound is only superficial.

**Harry:**    What? *(Into his mobile)* Hello Ambulance – sorry, I'm cancelling again because the wound is only superficial.

**Paudge:**    *(Still blinking)* Ah Jaysas – my eyes are full of bits of meringue.

**Harry:**    *(Angrily into the phone)* Yes, I am the same gobshite that phoned about the water in the tap – what do you want, a written apology? *(Clicks off)* What the hell is going on here?

**Jimmy:**    Harry, it wasn't my fault ...

**Harry:**    I know exactly who's fault it is – and by Christ he's not getting away with it ... *(Runs and grabs Maurice)* because you are the most twisted bastard I ever met – draggin' us through this to blame us all for things we didn't do ...

**Jimmy:**    *(Grabs Harry)* Let him go, Harry.

**Maurice:**    *(Furiously)* You did do them ... you did do them ...

**Deirdre:** Will you stop shouting ...

**Harry:** We shaggin' didn't – I don't know what you did after we left but we did shaggin' nothing ...

**Jimmy:** *(Holding Harry)* Harry!

**Maurice:** Yes you did but you won't admit it – I did nothing, I was only untying him, why did he call me a pervert, I was only untying him, it wasn't me that was the pervert ...

**Harry:** *(Furiously grabs Maurice again)* Are you saying I'm a pervert now – is this the next on your shaggin' programme, have you films of this too ... ?

**Jimmy:** Harry, you'll kill him ... *(Pulls Harry back)*

**Maurice:** Just admit he haunted you the way he haunted me ...

**Harry:** *(Grabs and shakes Maurice)* He didn't – and will you, for Christ's sake, get it into your twisted brain once and for all that we didn't cause Gregory's death, it wasn't our fault and whether we like it or not, Gregory is now dead dead dead, he's in his grave, he won't be coming back, we'll never see him again and none of it is our fault!

*(During this – as thunder cracks and lightning flashes across the room, flickering the lights – the door has opened and a boy of 17 stands looking in. Jackie sees him first and screams)*

**Jackie:** Oh my God, who is that?

**Harry:** *(Cries out)* Oh Jesus – it's Gregory!

*(All turn to see him and immediately we go to darkness)*

END OF SCENE ONE, ACT TWO

# ACT TWO
# SCENE TWO

*It is ten minutes later. The storm has abated: occasional distant rumbles and some lightning.*

*Maurice is carefully re-packing his projector and his films. Jimmy is collecting the many empty bottles and putting them into plastic bags. Harry is on his mobile. The discarded broken film lies on the floor.*

*The boy – Kevin – watches them: annoyed and authoritative. He has been reproaching them constantly – and is still talking as the lights come up.*

Kevin:      *(Angrily)* By right I should call the cops for all of you ...

Harry:      *(Into his mobile)* Speak up, Paul.

Kevin:      ... my da told me the first thing I should do if anyone ever phoned to say there was someone in the school, was *not* to come in – I mean you're lucky it's not my da who's here tonight because he always says first call the cops because they could be junkies or skinheads or spacers stoned out of their skulls – in fact, the only reason I came in is that I thought you were just a gang of kids coming home from the disco, not a crowd of oul fellas fighting with each other ...

Harry:      *(Furious at Kevin)* Hey Mick, John or whatever your name is ...

Kevin:      *(Hard)* It's Kevin!

Harry:      Well, Kevin, would you ever shut-up – I'm trying to do business here ...

Kevin:      *(Loudly)* No, I won't shut-up – you're not supposed to be in here and I told you ten minutes ago ...

Harry:      *(Angrily)* And we're not deaf – just keep it down for two minutes. *(Into his mobile)* Sorry, Paul, the son of the caretaker is getting very bolshie here.

**Kevin:**     And you say that again and you're out *now* – and
          your yuppie telephone after you. And where's the
          rest gone? – I don't want any of you rambling
          around the building.

**Maurice:**   Please – the ladies are simply looking after the in-
          jured gentlemen ...

**Kevin:**     And that's another thing – injuries. My da is tak-
          ing no responsibility for any injuries ...

**Maurice:**   No one is asking him to. They will be back here
          soon and then we will be going – all right?

**Kevin:**     Okay.

**Harry:**     (*Into this mobile*) The three o'clock flight would be
          great, Paul ... (*Listens*)

**Kevin:**     (*Now quieter. Curious*) Not that I want to know or
          anything – but what was it anyway? – some kind
          of party?

**Maurice:**   It was a coming to terms.

**Kevin:**     A what?

**Maurice:**   A reunion – and a very successful one at that.

**Kevin:**     (*Looks around*) Oh right. And the two women – did
          you pick them up or what?

**Maurice:**   Those ladies are the wives of the gentlemen here!

**Kevin:**     Oh. (*Then*) So if you didn't get the women in,
          what was it: booze, drugs, messing – like, are they
          blue movies that you were showing while ... ?

**Maurice:**   (*Adamant*) Our evening was one dedicated to ex-
          amining our lives, to chatting about old times, to
          remembering things past, to watching some nos-
          talgic silent films and next we were going to have
          our communal sing-song.

**Kevin:**     Oh Jaysas – the wild bunch.
          (*A distant roll of thunder as Jackie comes in*)

**Jackie:**    This building would give you the creeps.

**Maurice:**   Is Nick all right, Jackie?

**Jackie:**    He's fine. We got the First Aid box from the car –
          I'm really glad Deirdre was here.

**Kevin:**     (*Aggressive again*) None of you should be here at
          all.

Jackie:      We know – and you gave us a dreadful fright walking in like that.

Kevin:       It happens to be my job to walk in like that.

Jackie:      And you're sure I didn't see you down the corridor about twenty minutes ago ...

Kevin:       Yes I am, but you see me now – and in five minutes I don't want to see any of you – I want this place cleared. Where's the rest of them?

Jackie:      They're coming! They're coming!

Harry:       *(Into his mobile)* Okay, see you in the morning, Paul and thanks for everything tonight. *(Clicks off)*

Kevin:       *(Going)* Five minutes and if you're not all gone, it's the cops. *(Goes)*

Maurice:     Jackie, I must say I'm awfully sorry for what happened to Nick ...

Harry:       *(Angrily)* Nick? It's not just Nick, it's all of us – you walked us into this with that shaggin' programme ...

Jackie:      Oh not again!

Maurice:     No Harry, I honestly feel it was very successful ...

Harry:       Successful? I got belted against the wall, Nick got stabbed, Paudge thought his eyes were burned out, Jimmy could've been up for murder – that's your idea of successful, is it?

Maurice:     Harry, it did get us to face up to ...

Harry:       Oh Christ, I've had enough of this ...

Maurice:     No Harry, Gregory's parents told me all about the holiday you offered them after he ...

Harry:       *(Stops)* I'm a travel agent – I offer everybody holidays ...

Maurice:     And I know you've never forgotten him, you visit his grave ...

Harry:       I never even thought of him until you ...

Maurice:     No, when that boy walked in you shouted 'Gregory' as if ...

Harry:       That's it! *(Grabs a bag of bottles)* Here Jimmy, I'll help you take these down.

Maurice:     It's all right, Harry – I saw his face in the seminary, Jimmy sees him in his dreams ...

**Jimmy:**    I do not and don't you start on me again. (*Picks up the other bag*)

**Harry:**    (*Furiously*) You know, you really should have gone on to be a priest – and then joined the shaggin' Spanish Inquisition.

**Jimmy:**    Exactly.

(*Jimmy and Harry go with the bags*)

**Maurice:**  (*To Jackie*) It takes time.

**Jackie:**   Was it really so bad, Maurice?

**Maurice:**  In his diary, Gregory only called it 'The Incident'. And his last words, written on the day he died, were 'I am not, I am not'. (*Paudge comes in*) Ah Paudge, is your face all right?

**Paudge:**   Yes – I gave it a good wash. I'm glad you're still here, Jackie.

(*Maurice goes to the other room to collect his tools and plug connectors*)

**Jackie:**   I'll be gone as soon as Nick comes back.

**Paudge:**   You threw the film to me, Jackie – that was like old times.

**Jackie:**   What?

**Paudge:**   And then you ran over to me, all panicky and concerned, when you thought Nick had blinded me.

**Jackie:**   Oh for God's sake!

**Paudge:**   And you know all about him now, don't you – Gregory and the lipstick and all that ...

**Jackie:**   (*Annoyed*) Yes and so what?

**Paudge:**   So what? Does that not tell you exactly what he is?

**Jackie:**   I know what he is.

**Paudge:**   Okay – and you also know what we had together, you and me ...

**Jackie:**   Oh I do!

**Paudge:**   So, without any commitment, why don't we arrange to just meet and talk and maybe ...

**Jackie:**   Paudge, you left me when I was pregnant ...

**Paudge:**  Jackie, I'm talking about *now*.

**Jackie:**  And now there is Nick – he cares for me, he cares for Emma ...

**Paudge:**  But it's not what you want, Jackie – it's only a half-life.

**Jackie:**  *(Furious)* Paudge, it's *my* life – and what I want right now, more than anything else in this world, is for you to stay out of it!

**Paudge:**  *(Angrily)* All right – then if I can't see you, I have a right to see Emma.

**Jackie:**  You have no rights.

**Paudge:**  She's my daughter.

**Jackie:**  Sure of that, are you?

**Paudge:**  What?

**Jackie:**  Well don't be – don't ever be.

**Paudge:**  *(Furious)* What the hell do you mean by that?
*(Deirdre comes in with Nick. He is stripped to the waist. His wound is expertly bandaged)*

**Maurice:**  *(Coming from the room)* Ah Nick – feeling all right?

**Nick:**  Yes. Getting my clothes. Then we'll be going, Jackie.

**Jackie:**  All right Nick. *(Helps him with his clothes)*

**Deirdre:**  He won't need stitches or anything – but he should see a doctor tomorrow.

**Jackie:**  Thanks Deirdre – you've been wonderful.
*(Harry and Jimmy come in)*

**Jimmy:**  *(Brightly)* Ah Deirdre, everything all right?

**Deirdre:**  With Nick, yes.

**Jimmy:**  Just like to say I'm very proud of what you did.

**Deirdre:**  Which is more than I can say about you.

**Jimmy:**  What?

**Deirdre:**  Maurice, I was thinking, if you want me to look in at your father some evening or even for a night or two, I'd be happy to do that.

**Jimmy:**  Deirdre!

**Maurice:**  Oh that's very kind, Deirdre.

**Deirdre:**  Give you a little break – and I could wear my nurses uniform, make it official ... because I don't

think I'll be needing it for anything else, after
tonight.

**Maurice:** Well thank you, Deirdre – I think he'd like the
female company.

**Deirdre:** Grand. And some people can forget all about their
Florence Nightingales and their Firemen and their
tins of meringues.

**Nick:** Okay, we're off.

**Jackie:** I'll drive, darling.

**Paudge:** Jackie, don't go without saying if you meant what
you said.

**Nick:** Said? What was said?

**Jackie:** Tell you later, Nick – come on.

**Paudge:** Jackie, that's all I have left.

**Maurice:** *(At the blackboard)* Ladies, gentlemen. Apaches –
don't end the night like this: I know there are
things we all found out about each other and
about ourselves ...

**Nick:** *(Moving)* Right, Jackie?

**Maurice:** Please Nick! So now, to end our first Apache reunion, why don't we show a bit of solidarity by ...

**Harry:** You're not suggesting the shaggin' sing-song
now, are you?

**Maurice:** It's on the programme, Harry, it's on the blackboard and it would be nice to ...

**Harry:** *(Furiously)* Programme! Let me at that shaggin'
programme ...
*(Harry rips the programme off the wall. Maurice tries
to stop him)*

**Maurice:** No Harry, I want to keep that ...

**Harry:** It's been the ruination of this night ... and so have
you ...

**Maurice:** No Harry ...
*(Harry has grabbed Maurice. Immediately Nick,
Jimmy and Paudge run to keep them apart. In the
sudden confrontation, Kevin runs in. He has a stick
which he crashes onto a desk)*

**Kevin:** Okay, okay, okay – out!

*(He slams the stick onto the desk again. All stop)*

**Kevin:** Come on, out of this room, out of this school now and I mean now! *(Slams the stick down again)* You're only a shower of messers and I've had enough – so out, come on, out!

*(Harry, Nick, Paudge, Jimmy and Maurice now stand together to face him)*

**Harry:** *(Calm annoyance)* Just a shaggin' minute, sonny.

**Kevin:** Don't you 'sonny' me.

**Harry:** It so happens we have every right to be here.

**Kevin:** Don't you start ...

**Harry:** It so happens we all went to this school – we all sat in this very classroom ...

**Jimmy:** That's right, we put our names up over that window ...

**Harry:** You can have a look – they're still there ...

**Nick:** *(Unification)* That's right – and when we were here, we ran this classroom ...

**Harry:** It was we that told kids like you what to do and where to go ...

**Paudge:** *(Unification)* And nobody argued with us.

**Nick:** This place belonged to us.

**Kevin:** *(Pause. Then)* Big deal – well I was in this school too, in this classroom up to three months ago – I sat over there by that wall ...

**Harry:** That's where I sat ... by the wall.

**Nick:** I sat beside him ...

**Paudge:** I was behind them ...

**Jimmy:** Did you ever hear of Brother Holmes?

**Kevin:** Sherlock?

**Nick:** Yes, we called him that too.

**Kevin:** Sherlock is okay – he's the superior in the new school.

**Harry:** Oh yeah, Sherlock was okay.

**Jimmy:** Yeah, I personally liked him.

**Maurice:** *(To Kevin)* Did you ever hear of a boy called Gregory?

*(All suddenly move)*

| | |
|---|---|
| **Nick:** | Okay Harry, lads – we're off. Take care. |
| **Harry:** | Okay Nick – you keep in touch, give me a bell sometime, on the mobile. |
| **Nick:** | Will do. *(Going)* |
| **Maurice:** | It all went well, Nick. |
| **Jackie:** | Deirdre, call in at the shop sometime. |
| **Deirdre:** | I will, Jackie, and thanks. |
| **Paudge:** | Jackie ... ? |
| **Jackie:** | *(Continuing to Deirdre)* We'll have a nice chat. *(Goes)* |
| **Paudge:** | *(Calls)* You know where I am, Jackie. *(Nick looks at Paudge and follows Jackie)* |
| **Maurice:** | *(Picks up his projector)* Well until the next Apache reunion, gentlemen. |
| **Harry:** | Oh sure – I can't wait for it! |
| **Paudge:** | Will you be able to manage all that stuff, Maurice? |
| **Maurice:** | I think so. |
| **Paudge:** | I'll carry the suitcase for you. |
| **Maurice:** | Many thanks, Paudge. |
| **Deirdre:** | Bye Paudge – and I'll be seeing you soon, Maurice. |
| **Maurice:** | Many thanks, Deirdre. And Jimmy, I think we'll all sleep better now. |
| **Jimmy:** | *(Quietly)* Oh will we? |
| **Maurice:** | And Harry, next year, my house – I'll be insisting on it. *(Paudge and Maurice go)* |
| **Kevin:** | Okay, I'm turning out the lights now. |
| **Deirdre:** | We're going. Bye Harry. |
| **Harry:** | Yeah, see you, Deirdre – and I gave you my card didn't I? – special deals for the kids. |
| **Deirdre:** | Oh yes – thanks. *(Going)* |
| **Jimmy:** | *(Following)* Deirdre, you're forgetting your meringue tin. |
| **Deirdre:** | If you want it, you get it. *(Goes)* |
| **Jimmy:** | *(Picks up the tin. Awkwardly to Harry)* Women – she'll be looking for that later. *(Goes)* *(Harry, as he turns to go, looks around. Kevin watches* |

*him)*

| | |
|---|---|
| **Harry:** | Great oul school. |
| **Kevin:** | Shaggin' kip. I'm glad it's being pulled down. |
| **Harry:** | Don't think we are – too many ghosts. |
| **Kevin:** | Were you all supposed to be mates or something? |
| **Harry:** | Oh yeah. We were known as the Apaches here – as I say, nobody messed with us. |
| **Kevin:** | *(Amused)* Oh yeah? |
| **Harry:** | Yeah – for example they called me Crazy Horse. |
| **Kevin:** | *(Amused)* Jaysas! |
| **Harry:** | *(Annoyed)* And there was a very good reason why I was called that – good reasons why we all had our names: we were pretty rough guys here ... there was nobody that wasn't afraid of us. Nobody! |
| **Kevin:** | And who was Gregory? |

*(From now, very gradually, an image appears on the back wall, as though through a projector. At first, barely noticeable, it slowly becomes clearer. It is of a schoolboy, facing us, unsmiling. In the distance, the rumble of thunder)*

| | |
|---|---|
| **Harry:** | *(Stops)* What? |
| **Kevin:** | Gregory. Was he the oul fella with the glasses? |
| **Harry:** | No no, that wasn't Gregory. Gregory wasn't here tonight – because Gregory is dead. |
| **Kevin:** | He's dead? |
| **Harry:** | Yeah. *(Then. With difficulty)* A long time ago, me and the other Apaches, we killed him. |
| **Kevin:** | *(Dubious and amused)* You killed him? |

*(Harry picks up the discarded 'Woods' film from the floor and puts it into his pocket)*

| | |
|---|---|
| **Harry:** | *(Then)* That's right. That's why we were all here tonight: to sit around and talk about it, watch a film about it, to remember exactly what we did and how we did it. Okay? |
| **Kevin:** | *(Still amused)* Oh sure – okay. |
| **Harry:** | See you around, Kevin. *(Goes)* |
| **Kevin:** | Yeah see you. *(Calls)* And hey, that's cool – I like |

it. *(Then to himself)* Ya bleedin' spoofer – you must think I'm a right thick to believe that.

*(Already we hear the recording of 'Running Bear' as Kevin throws the stick aside, turns out the lights and leaves.*

*The image on the wall is now very clear and immediately begins to fade ... as the music gets louder to the end)*

### THE END

# APPENDIX

Suggested shooting script for Maurice's film:

**Scene 1: Ext. Powerscourt Stream. Day:**
Establish Powerscourt. Now a close shot of Harry, Nick, Jimmy, Paudge and Jackie – arms around each other. Much waving to camera.

Now, they cross the stream by the stones – Harry in control, tries to push Jimmy in. Nick looking very fashionable. Paudge holding Jackie's hand. She wears her straw hat.

**Scene 2: Ext. Powerscourt Green Area:**
Jimmy, unaware of the camera, stands alone. He is examining a dead hedgehog. Establish. Now Jimmy becomes aware of the camera. Smiles in embarrassment, hiding the hedgehog.

**Scene 3: Ext. Powerscourt Downstream:**
Trying to cross the stream by the swinging rope. Nick very assured. Now all sitting on the bank, watching him. He falls in. Disgusted – he now realises the camera is watching. Now light-hearted – splashes the others.

**Scene 4: Ext. Powerscourt. Secluded Area:**
The camera creeps along and finds Paudge and Jackie kissing. They see him. Tell him to go away. He won't. Jackie holds her straw hat up to conceal them from the camera's prying eye.

**Scene 5: Ext. Powerscourt Car-Park:**
Everyone running from the camera, some falling and then running on. Looking back. Jackie and Paudge hand-in-hand. Now all looking back and shouting 'Look out, behind you'. Suddenly the camera goes wild: Maurice having been caught

and thumped.

## Scene 6: Powerscourt. Field Area:

Jackie and Paudge sit on a grass verge, watching Nick, Harry and Jimmy doing the established 'Apache Dance'. Great enthusiasm for this.

At the end of this dance, Harry and Jimmy and Nick stand arm in arm. Paudge and Jackie join them for this group shot. On this, the film goes to blank.

# THREE PLAYS
## Sharon's Grave, The Crazy Wall, The Man from Clare

### John B. Keane

Like John B. Keane's hugely successful play and subsequent film of *The Field*, *Sharon's Grave* deals with man's ruthless lust for land, which overrides all familial loyalties, and can ultimately lead to tragedy.

In *The Crazy Wall*, John B. Keane has lost none of his realistic force in creating the powerful symbol of the wall that Michael Barnett erects – ostensibly to ward off tramps and other interlopers – but in fact for deeper, intensely personal reasons known only to himself. Is this wall intended to serve as a moat, to isolate Michael from the harsh realities of the outside world? Or does it symbolise for Michael and the members of his family, the lack of communication between them that sometimes make a husband and wife, brothers and sisters seem like strangers under the same roof.

*The Man from Clare* deals with the personal tragedy of an ageing athlete who finds he no longer has the physical strength to maintain his position as captain of the team, or his reputation as the best footballer in Clare.

# MOLL

## John B. Keane

*Moll* is John B. Keane's hilarious and highly successful comedy about life in an Irish country presbytery.

'When a presbytery gets a new housekeeper it becomes like a country that gets a change of government, or like a family that gets a new stepmother.' Moll Kettle would work for no less than a canon for, in her own words, ''Tis hard to come back to the plain black and white when one is used to the purple'.

# THE YEAR OF THE HIKER

## John B. Keane

'*The Year of the Hiker* is among the best of Keane's dramas, sinewy and engrossing, and a realistic piece of storytelling ...'

EVENING HERALD

The Hiker is the much hated father who deserted his wife and family and whose return is awaited with fear.

# THREE PLAYS
## Sive, The Field, Big Maggie

### John B. Keane

*Sive* is a powerful folk-drama set in the north-west of Ireland which concerns itself with the attempt of a scheming matchmaker and a bitter woman to sell an innocent young girl to a lecherous old man.

*The Field* is John B. Keane's fierce and tender study of the love a man can have for land and the ruthless lengths he will go to in order to obtain the object of his desire.

*Big Maggie:* On the death of her husband Maggie is determined to create a better life for herself and her children. The problems arise when her vision of the future begins to sit with increasing discomfort on the shoulders of her surly offspring. John B. Keane's wonderful creation of a rural Irish matriarch ranks with Juno, Mommo and Molly Bloom as one of the great female creations of twentieth-century Irish literature.

# THE CHASTITUTE

## John B. Keane

'A Chastitute is a person without holy orders who has never lain down with a woman ... a rustic celibate by force of circumstance peculiar to countrysides where the Catholic tradition of long-life sexual abstemiousness is encouraged ... free-range sex is absolutely taboo ...'

John Bosco, who hasn't the 'makings of a dacent sin in him', is a bachelor farmer and all he is searching for is a plain decent woman to share his life. He 'nearly got there a thousand times but nearly never bulled a cow'. The two things which militated most against his endeavours with the opposite sex were Missionaries and Townies.